AIR VANGUARD 17

VOUGHT F4U CORSAIR

JAMES D'ANGINA

First published in Great Britain in 2014 by Osprey Publishing,
PO Box 883, Oxford, OX1 9PL, UK
1385 Broadway, 5th Floor, New York, NY 10018, USA
Email: info@ospreypublishing.com

Osprey Publishing is part of Bloomsbury Publishing Plc

A CIP catalog record for this book is available from the British Library.

Print ISBN: 978 1 78200 626 8
ePub ISBN: 978 178200 628 2
PDF eBook ISBN: 978 1 78200 627 5

Index by Sandra Shotter
Typeset in Sabon
Originated by PDQ Media, Bungay, UK
Printed in China through World Print Ltd.

18 19 20 21 22   11 10 9 8 7 6 5 4 3 2

Osprey Publishing is supporting the Woodland Trust, the UK's leading
woodland conservation charity, by funding the dedication of trees.

www.ospreypublishing.com

ACKNOWLEDGMENTS

I would like to thank the following individuals for their contribution towards this volume: Dr. Ian Spurgeon, military historian; Mr. Steve Smith, curator of the Flying Leatherneck Museum; Mr. Stephen Ove, 353d Special Operations Group, historian; Mr. Ben Kristy, aviation curator for the National Museum of the Marine Corps (NMMC); Carrier Bowers, museum specialist, NMMC; Mr. Mitch Garringer, head of the Restoration Department at the NMMC; Kara Newcomer, historian, Marine Corps History Division, Historical Reference Branch; Mr. Chris Ellis, Archives & Special Collections Branch, Library of the Marine Corps, Marine Corps History Division; Lt Col Robert Pekarek (USAF); Mr. Nate Patch, Archivist, National Archives, College Park; and the exhibit staff of the USS *Midway* Museum. Also, I would like to thank my family for their patience with me while writing this volume. Any errors found within this volume are the sole responsibility of the author.

CONTENTS

VOUGHT F4U CORSAIR

INTRODUCTION

The Vought F4U Corsair is considered one of the greatest fighters of World War II, excelling in its overall performance and adaptability to a variety of missions. While production of other comparable piston-engine fighters ended after World War II, the United States Navy and Marine Corps continued to have faith in the "bent wing bird" and procured new versions of the Corsair from Vought. Although designed in the late 1930s, the last Corsair came off the Vought production line in December 1952. The Corsair was introduced into combat at a crucial juncture in the Pacific campaign, giving the Allies an advantage over Japan's legendary Mitsubishi A6M Type Zero fighter and gaining the ability to fight on their own terms. One of the greatest testaments to the Corsair's primacy came not from Mr. Rex B. Beisel, considered the father of the Corsair, but from the chief engineer of the A6M Zero fighter, Dr Jiro Horikoshi, who said: "The Corsair was the first single-engine fighter which clearly surpassed the Zero in performance." The F4U received hundreds of design changes, improving the breed over time; this allowed the Corsair to maintain an edge over the best Japanese production fighters throughout the war. The Corsair's issues with carrier operations were eventually solved, and the F4U was later chosen as the standard carrier fighter over the Grumman F6F Hellcat. By war's end the Corsair was credited with destroying 2,140 Japanese aircraft in air-to-air combat while losing 189, giving the Corsair an impressive 11:1 air-to-air kill ratio against the Japanese.

The air-to-air engagements tell only part of the story. The Corsair's contribution as a fighter-bomber is even more impressive. The F4U was not designed nor intended to replace aircraft like the Douglas SBD Dauntless and SB2C Curtiss Helldiver on the decks of US Navy carriers, but the Corsair's ability to perform as a precision dive bomber nearly equaled that of the SBD Dauntless, considered one of the best naval dive bombers of the war. This should have come as little surprise, since Vought had vast experience in building scout bombers from the early Corsair biplanes and the SB2U Vindicator, from which the F4U traced its lineage. The F4U Corsair could carry more ordnance than the Douglas SBD, Grumman TBF Avenger, or the Curtiss SB2C Helldiver. The last model to see action during World War II, the F4U-4, had a maximum bomb load of 4,000lbs, comparable to the standard bomb load carried by Boeing B-17 Flying Fortresses on long-range missions over Europe.

During the Korean War, the Corsair once again demonstrated its worth, flying the majority of all US Navy and Marine Corps close-air support missions. The Corsair's ruggedness and reliability played a major role in the success of the Marine Corps close-air support system. As the war progressed, two new variants were produced to deal with the harsh conditions and combat faced in Korea: the F4U-5NL, an all-weather or winterized night fighter which incorporated de-icing equipment, and the AU-1 low-level ground-attack variant with additional armor and hard points. Although the Corsair was no longer considered as nor expected to serve as an air superiority fighter, Corsair pilots still managed to down enemy fighters, including the formidable MiG-15 (the only other piston-engine fighter to bring down a MiG-15 during the war was a Hawker Sea Fury). Interestingly, it was not the Grumman F9F Panther that would produce the Navy's only ace of the Korean War, but the veteran Corsair.

The Corsair's enviable combat record continued after the Korean War. The French Aeronavale chose to purchase a new version of the Corsair over designs like the Grumman Bearcat and the Hawker Sea Fury. French Aeronavale squadrons flew both AU-1s on loan from the US Navy and F4U-7 Corsairs purpose-built for French service during the First Indochina War. French Corsairs would see action in Algeria, Tunisia, and during Operation *Musketeer* (the Suez Crisis) in 1956. It was not until 1969 that the Corsair saw its dramatic end in combat. During the 100 Hours' War between El Salvador and Honduras, Corsairs on both sides saw service as fighter-bombers. Near the end of this conflict, a Honduran Corsair pilot shot down a Cavalier F-51D Mustang and two Goodyear-built Corsairs. This last recorded engagement between piston-engine fighters in combat concluded a legendary era of military aviation.

The cannon-equipped F4U-4B saw combat for the first time on July 3, 1950. Sixteen Corsairs from VF-53 and VF-54 were launched from the USS *Valley Forge* (CV-45) during the initial US Navy strike of the Korean War. This F4U-B Corsair from VF-54 prepares to launch from the "Happy Valley" in late 1950. (National Archives)

DESIGN AND DEVELOPMENT

The United States Navy began testing the first Corsair (bureau number A-7221) at Anacostia Naval Air Station on March 18, 1926. The test plane was not the F4U that comes to mind at the mention of the word Corsair but an observation aircraft (O2U), and the first of many Vought designs to carry the name that would become renowned. The O2U was given its nickname by Chance Vought in honor of his family's past ventures of building sailing ships. It was one of the first aircraft in the Navy to have a company nickname, a tradition that continues today. A revolutionary air-cooled Wasp R-1340 radial engine built by Pratt & Whitney powered the Corsair. The fuselage was streamlined and built from welded steel tubing. This combination allowed the Corsair to set multiple speed and altitude world records in its class. The O2U had flying qualities similar to contemporary single-seat pursuit aircraft. Internal armament consisted of a single .30cal fixed machine gun located in the top wing, a first for a US Navy aircraft. The observation seat located at the rear of the aircraft incorporated a flexible gun mount capable of carrying up to two .30cal machine guns. Vought built a total of 132 O2U Corsairs, including two prototypes for the Navy, Coast Guard, and Marine Corps at the company's Long Island NY facility. Chance Vought produced four separate models (O2U-1, 2, 3 and 4). The company also received orders from 13 foreign nations who operated the Corsair biplanes. The Corsair saw considerable action in Nicaragua with the Marines, most notably as the aircraft used by Marine aviator Lieutenant Christian Schilt to evacuate 18 wounded Marines in Quilali and thereby receive the Medal of Honor.

The O2U's success led to the creation of a two-seat fighter prototype, the XF2U-1. It featured an enclosed cowling that would be featured on later models of the Corsair. The sole prototype met the Bureau of Aeronautics requirements. However, ongoing O2U production slowed the development and in the end the Navy decided against the Vought two-seater aircraft. The next aircraft to carry the Corsair name was the Vought O3U. Similar to the O2U-4 in many respects, the O3U was the first complete aircraft to be tested in Langley Field's full-scale wind tunnel on May 27, 1931. The model entered naval service as an observation aircraft and Marine Corps use as a scout plane. Officials changed the aircraft's designation to SU-1 to better reflect its mission. The O3U-2 incorporated some significant changes, including a new R-1690 Pratt & Whitney Hornet engine, updated cockpit, and the elimination of the scarf ring mounts in the observer's seat. Later models relied on both Hornet and Wasp engines, and the final variant, the O3U-6, saw the inclusion of an enclosed cockpit.

XF3U-1 and SBU Corsair

In 1932, the Navy's Bureau of Aeronautics revisited the idea of procuring a two-seat fighter and released requirements for bids from the aviation industry. The Navy selected both Douglas and Vought to each build a single prototype. Vought's prototype, the XF3U-1, was designed by newly hired Rex Buren Beisel, who later led a team to create the F4U. The first flight of the XF3U-1 took place in May 1933. Powered by a Pratt & Whitney R-1535 Twin Wasp Jr engine, with a fully enclosed cowling and an enclosed cockpit, the aircraft's performance was similar to single-seat fighters. Aware that the Navy might abandon the two-seat fighter project, Vought pushed the idea of testing the XF3U-1 as a scout aircraft to replace SU Corsairs. The Bureau of Aeronautics agreed to test the aircraft in the scout role. When the Navy's two-seat fighter project was shelved, the Bureau of Aeronautics requested that Vought modify the XF3U-1 into a prototype scout bomber.

The F4U Corsair's ancestory traces back to one of Rex Beisel's early designs at Vought, the SBU-1 Corsair. The SBU-1 was originally developed as a two-seat fighter designated the XF3U-1. The Navy later requested the aircraft be modified into a scout-bomber. Vought instead built a new airframe and used parts from the XF3U-1 to create the XSBU-1. The SBU Corsair was the last biplane to be produced by Vought. (NMNA)

Vought decided to build an entirely new aircraft, though with components from the XF3U-1 in order to keep within the Navy's requirement. The aircraft, named the XSBU-1 Corsair, retained the same bureau number as the XF3U-1. The XF3U-1 took on a new bureau number and mission as a test aircraft. The design team developed larger and stronger wings, increased internal fuel capacity, and streamlined the fuselage. The new scout bomber incorporated a controllable pitch propeller and a cowling design tested by the National Advisory Committee for Aeronautics (NACA). One of the more innovative features was the use of adjustable cowl gills, which improved airflow over the cylinders. The SBU-1 Corsair was the first production aircraft to incorporate cowl gills/flaps. The cowl gills aided the SBU-1 in exceeding 200mph in level flight, a first for its class. Cowl flaps eventually became standard on most air-cooled radial engine designs. The SBU-1 Corsair was armed with two .30cal machine guns, one fixed and one moveable, and was capable of carrying a single 500lb bomb. The Navy ordered 84 SBU-1 Corsairs, receiving the first aircraft in November 1935. An additional 40 SBU-2 aircraft entered Navy service later. The SBU Corsairs remained in service with the Naval Reserves until 1941.

Beisel Designs

The US Navy sought to procure all-new scout and torpedo bombers at the end of 1934. Beisel, now the chief engineer at Vought, proposed a monoplane design with retractable landing gear, a first for the company. It became the SB2U Vindicator. The Navy officials met the XSB2U with some skepticism. Some officers within the Bureau of Aeronautics believed monoplane designs were ill-suited for carrier operations. Due to this concern, Vought would receive a second contract to build a prototype biplane to compete for the Navy's new scout bomber requirement. The biplane,

a heavily modified SBU Corsair, was designated the XSB3U. The biplane incorporated an even more streamlined engine cowling than the SBU, retractable landing gear, and a Pratt & Whitney R-1535 engine. In April 1936, the Navy flew comparison tests between Vought's two prototypes at Anacostia Naval Air Station.. The tests demonstrated the monoplane's superiority over the biplane design. The same engine powered both prototypes, and even though the monoplane was heavier than the biplane it was 15mph faster than the biplane prototype. The Navy requested Vought halt all work on the XSBU-3. Vought received an order for 54 examples of the SB2U-1 in October 1936, with the first being delivered to the Navy in December 1937. The following year the Navy ordered 58 SB2U-2s, and in 1940 ordered 57 of the final variant, the, the first in the series to use the name Vindicator.

The majority of SB2U-3 Vindicators were delivered to the Marines. Marine Vindicators were at Ewa during the attack on Pearl Harbor, and saw action against the Japanese during the Battle of Midway in June 1942. Of the 170 built at the Stratford Connecticut plant, only one survived for display purposes: SB2U-2 (BuNo 1378), the last SB2U delivered to the Navy, resides at the National Museum of Naval Aviation in Pensacola, Florida.

Request for Proposals

In February 1938, the United States Navy's Bureau of Aeronautics released a request for proposals to the aviation industry for a carrier-borne fighter of both single-engine and twin-engine designs. The performance requirements set forth by the Navy for the new single-engine fighter were well beyond the reach of the day's production aircraft. This common practice forced the aircraft industry to respond with innovative designs rather than just updated versions of past models. Chief Engineer Rex Beisel headed up the team that submitted Vought's design proposal. Vought submitted two designs on April 8, 1938, which were both aimed towards the single-engine request, and both were projected to be powered by Pratt & Whitney radial engines. The V-166A was proposed to be powered by an R-1830 Twin Wasp and the V-166B powered by the prototype XR-2800 Double Wasp air-cooled radial engine producing 1,850 horsepower. Although the proposal drew upon past Vought designs (including features such as its 90-degree gear rotation, empennage, and folding wings mechanism), it was unlike anything Vought had built previously.

The Competition

Four companies besides Vought submitted proposals. These included Grumman, Curtiss, Brewster Aeronautical Corporation, and Bell. Grumman submitted proposals for both the single- and twin-engine requirements, winning the later. Their single engine submission was an updated version of the Wildcat, powered by an R-2600 engine. Brewster's proposals aimed at the

Navy's single engine requirement, and their designs had the option to be powered by either an R-2600 or XR-2800 engine. Curtiss offered up a navalized version of the P-36 Mohawk, with an option to be powered by the R-1830 Twin Wasp or an R-2600 engine. Bell submitted a unique design based on the P-39 Airacobra. Their proposal was the only design to be powered by a liquid-cooled Allison V-1710 engine.

After evaluation by the Bureau of Aeronautics, the Navy found Vought's V-166B submission the best overall proposal to meet their single-engine requirement. On June 11, 1938, Vought received an order to build a single prototype based on the V-166B proposal. The Navy designated it the XF4U-1. The Navy was still interested in both the Brewster and Bell proposals and authorized both companies to build a single prototype each. Brewster failed to deliver due to internal issues, but Bell completed a navalized version of their P-39 named the XFL-1 Aero Bonita. The aircraft featured conventional landing gear for the time, instead of the P-39's tricycle gear, and a larger wing with folding mechanisms. The XFL's performance fared poorly against the XF4U-1, however, and the Navy lost interest in the project. The Navy's original goals succeeded; proposals based on older designs were less attractive than a new design. Vought, which had not delivered a single-seat fighter to the Navy since its FU series in the 1920s, was back to building fighters.

The XF4U-1, BuNo 1443, set a world speed record for a single engine fighter, reaching 405mph on October 1, 1940. The prototype's armament consisted of one .50cal and one .30cal machine gun, both firing out of the engine cowling, and one .50cal in each wing. A small compartment in each wing housed antiaircraft bombs intended for use against enemy bomber formations. (NMNA)

The XF4U-1

Beisel's design team strove to combine the strongest power plant available with the smallest fuselage and most streamlined airframe; Vought did so in hopes of meeting the Navy's most important requirement, "speed, speed, and more speed!" To streamline the aircraft, Vought utilized advanced techniques, including spot-welding and flush-riveting to minimize drag. To maximize

Vought test pilot Boone T. Guyton, seen at Stratford, Connecticut, in 1942, prepares for a flight in a F4U-1. Early production model F4U-1s had framed canopies (also called a bird cage); later F4U-1s were fitted with a raised piece of plexiglass incorporated into the top of the bird-cage canopy to house a rearview mirror. (NMNA)

Vought's engineers strove to design a streamlined airframe around the world's most powerful powerplant, Pratt & Whitney's XR-2800. To maximize the power of the new engine, the Corsair required a 13-foot-4-inch diameter Hamilton Standard three-bladed hydromatic aluminum propeller. (National Museum of the Marine Corps)

power from the XR-2800, the XF4U-1 utilized a 13-foot 4-inch diameter three-bladed hydromatic aluminum propeller built by Hamilton Standard. The size of the propeller, the largest fitted to a single-engine fighter at that time, required an innovative approach to the shape of the wing, one that took Vought engineers countless hours to develop. Beisel chose an inverted gull wing, allowing enough ground clearance for the propeller while providing the XF4U-1 with shorter main landing gear than with a more traditional wing design. An additional benefit to the inverted gull wing design was its 90-degree orientation position to the fuselage, permitting the least amount of aerodynamic drag while eliminating the need for wing fairings. The landing gear retracted aft within the wing knuckles, allowing the wings to be folded vertically, similar to the Vindicator. The streamlined circular cross section of the engine was accomplished by utilizing Beisel's advanced work into cooling methods. The design incorporated the air intakes for the supercharger and oil cooler within the leading edge of the wings. The XF4U-1 had fully enclosed main landing gear and retracting tail wheel and arrestor hook to minimize drag.

The Corsair prototype featured the world's most powerful radial engine of the time, the Pratt & Whitney XR-2800 Double Wasp. The XR-2800 engine was a radial design that had 18 cylinders set in two rows (nine each). The engine was air-cooled and utilized a two-stage, two-speed supercharger. The prototype XF4U-1 (BuNo 1443) was the first of many US aircraft to be powered by a Double Wasp engine (other notable fighters include the Republic P-47 Thunderbolt and the Grumman F6F Hellcat). The XF4U-1 was originally powered by an R2800-2, and later fitted with an R-2800-4 powerplant that produced 1,850 horsepower at takeoff.

The XF4U-1 had an armament arrangement consistent with the original Navy requirement: four machine guns (one .30cal machine gun and one .50cal firing out of the engine cowling through the prop arc, and one .50cal in each wing). The XF4U-1 also had compartments in each wing to house small antiaircraft bombs, which were intended for use against enemy bomber formations.

Chance Vought's chief test pilot, Lyman Bullard, flew the prototype Corsair (BuNo 1443) for the first time on May 29, 1940. Bullard had experienced a problem during the inaugural flight as the elevator trim tabs came loose in flight, but he made an uneventful landing back at Bridgeport with a number of VIPs in the crowd, and the elevator trim tabs were redesigned. Two test pilots, Bullard and Boone Guyton, would put the XF4U-1 through its paces prior to the Navy's acceptance trials. On July 9, 1940, Guyton flew the XF4U-1 for the first time; two days later the prototype was involved in a crash under the controls of the new test pilot. While testing the XF4U-1, Guyton ran into some bad weather and inadvertently ran low on fuel, forcing him to make an emergency landing on a golf course and causing serious damage to the sole prototype. It took three months to piece it back together. Testing the XF4U-1 continued. One improvement that took a considerable amount of time was restructuring the ailerons to give the Corsair better roll rates. Vought's persistence in finding the right size paid off, as the Corsair had tremendous roll rates even at high speeds. The bent wing bird nearly killed Guyton a second time during spin testing. Prior to the test, BuNo 1443 was fitted with an emergency chute in the tail. During the test Guyton was unable to get the Corsair out of a flat spin; Bullard reminded him to use the emergency chute over the radio, and with the chute deployed Guyton was able to recover and fly another day. Guyton would later go on to fly the first production F4U-1 Corsair off the assembly line, and he became indispensably linked to the Corsair. On October 1, 1940, Bullard set a world speed record in the XF4U-1 when he reached 405mph in level flight, a first for a single-engine fighter.

Requirement Changes

The Navy was so impressed with Vought's prototype that a formal request was issued to Chance Vought to build a production model on November 28, 1940. This was followed by an order for 584 examples of the new fighter on June 30, 1941, designated F4U-1. The Navy's requirement changed dramatically due to lessons being learned in Europe. This meant the addition of armor protection, self-sealing fuel tanks, and a heavier armament in the production model. The additional requirements would drastically change the appearance of the production-model Corsair from its prototype. The internal bomb compartments located in each wing were removed from the production model and the main armament was changed to six .50cal machine guns, three in each wing. The armament change displaced the fuel cells located in the wings, so the fuel cells were consolidated into one main fuel cell placed in the forward fuselage between the engine and the cockpit, making it necessary to move the cockpit three feet aft. Placing the main fuel tank (237 gallons) in the forward fuselage lengthened the Corsair's nose to 12 feet in front of the cockpit. This adversely affected the pilot's forward and downward view, making it difficult to conduct a carrier landing. The first production F4U-1 Corsair (BuNo 02153) was flown on June 25, 1942. The first production F4U-1s were delivered to the Navy in July of the same year.

Corsair Assembly

Vought reconfigured its Kingfisher assembly line at its Stratford plant to build the new Corsairs. The line needed to be completely reorganized and simplified for a less experienced workforce. Each Corsair was assembled from eight main assemblies, while the company subcontracted out multiple sub-assemblies. The main assemblies included the powerplant, three separate fuselage assemblies (forward, center, and aft), two wing assemblies (inner wing and outer wing), landing gear, and tail surfaces. The main beam was the keystone of the Corsair design. It had three sections of its own and was made from aluminum alloy to ensure lightness and strength. The main beam had to withstand heavy loads and formed the foundation for the inner wing section, giving the Corsair its inverted gull wing shape. The main beam

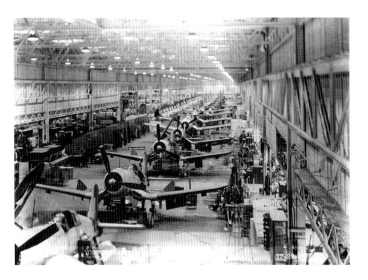

F4U-1 Corsairs on the final assembly line at the Vought-Sikorsky plant, December 23, 1942. Subcontracted Corsairs built by the Brewster Aeronautical Corporation were assembled in Johnsville, Pennsylvania, while Corsairs built by Goodyear Aircraft Corporation were produced on assembly lines in Akron, Ohio. (NMNA)

also supported a variety of other components, such as the main landing gear, the lower engine mount fittings, intercoolers, and the catapult hooks. The main beam was a complicated design, produced at a time when skilled labor was leaving the work force to go off to war. To ease production of the main beam, Vought built specially-designed drill and assembly jigs.

The Corsair assembly line was formed utilizing three lines, two loop lines and one final assembly line that ran the length of the plant. With a total of 71 assembly stations, technicians at each station had a set time to complete their work. The inner loop joined the middle and aft fuselage sections. The outer loop joined the inner wing section and the forward fuselage. These two U-shaped assembly lines ended a short distance from the start of the final assembly line. The final assembly started with the forward fuselage and wing section to ensure this area was still relatively accessible. The cockpit was installed, as well as electrical and hydraulic systems. The next stage joined the aft fuselage section to the forward section utilizing bolts, and also added the powerplant, outer wings, and landing gear. The canopy, gear doors, induction system, armor, and main fuel cell followed. The hydraulic system was checked to include wing folding, oil-cooler doors, cowl flaps, and landing-gear retraction. Once all the checks and tests were completed the aircraft was towed from the plant to adjacent Bridgeport Airport for flight tests. Vought's team of test pilots grew as production increased. Each Corsair had to be flight-tested; these checks would typically take two hours to complete, which was done prior to the plane's release to a naval aviator for delivery.

F4U-1 Production Inspection and Carrier Trials

A series of flight tests were carried out by the Navy starting in July 1942 to determine the Corsair's performance and handling characteristics, and to ascertain if the aircraft was suitable for service use. The initial production Corsair BuNo 02153 was the first aircraft involved with the tests, and was flown from Stratford, Connecticut to Anacostia Naval Air Station, District of Columbia, on July 21 1942, for preliminary tests. A second Corsair, BuNo

CORSAIR PROFILES
1. F4U-1 BuNo 02153, Stratford, Connecticut, 15 July 1942
This Corsair was the first production model
2. F4U-1A BuNo 17744, of VMF-214, Maj Gregory Boyington, Vella Lavella,
23 December 1943
3. F4U-1A BuNo 50341, Corsair II, JT537, of 1836 Sqn, Sub Lt Donald J. Sheppard,
HMS *Victorious*, May 1945
4. FG-1D BuNo 76236, Corsair IV, KD658, of 1841 Sqn, Sub Lt Robert H. Gray,
HMS *Formidable*, 1945

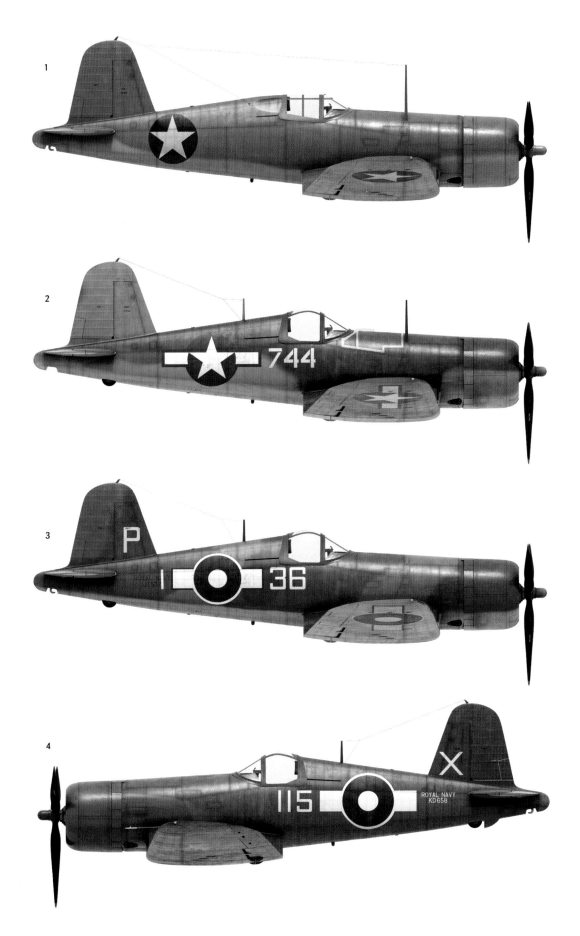

Armorers inspect an F4U-1's port machine guns prior to a boresighting test. The aircraft's tail section has been lifted off the ground by a field-constructed apparatus built from coconut logs. This F4U-1, named "Bubbles," was assigned to VMF-213 while on Guadalcanal. (National Archives)

02155, was used for the majority of performance tests and was delivered to Anacostia in April 1943. Corsair (BuNo 02555) was utilized to carry out drop-tank tests to aid in increasing the range of the fighter. Multiple Corsairs from the earliest production to modified-clipped wing F4Us and F4U-1D fighter-bomber variants were involved with these tests that lasted until September 1944.

On September 25, 1942, the eighth Corsair off the production line (BuNo 02160) took part in the initial carrier landing trials. Vought representatives were on board the escort carrier USS *Sangamon* CVE-26, positioned in the Chesapeake Bay, to witness the trial. Pilot Lieutenant Commander Sam Porter was the first to attempt a carrier landing. During his four landings and takeoffs, he noted several complications with the Corsair. The pilot had poor visibility from the cockpit while on approach, and leaking hydraulic fluid from the cowl flap actuators and engine oil splattered the windscreen. The short tail wheel raised the aircraft's nose significantly while taxiing, limiting the pilot's view of his surroundings and hindering directional control on the ground. Due to its rigid landing gear oleos, the Corsair had a tendency to bounce on landing. The Corsair also had an undesirable stall characteristic at approach speeds. The port wing would stall before the starboard wing due to the torque of the engine. This was especially apparent during carrier approaches.

Vought engineers wasted no time trying to alleviate the Corsair's carrier issues. They reduced the landing bounce over time by experimenting with pressure levels in the oleos struts. To improve visibility, Vought batted down the top three cowl flaps to eliminate fluid on the windscreen and raised the tail wheel six inches. Every solution developed by engineers was recorded in a master change log, used by all three companies producing Corsairs (Vought, Brewster, and Goodyear). On October 3, 1942, before all discrepancies had been fixed, the Navy's first operational Corsair squadron, VF-12, took delivery of its first F4U-1 Corsair. Led by Lieutenant Commander Joseph C. Clifton, VF-12 pilots qualified with the Corsair during carrier operations aboard the USS *Saratoga*. Adoption of the new Corsair proved costly, as the squadron lost 14 pilots in training accidents. The squadron would exchange their Corsairs for Grumman F6F Hellcats due to the lack of Corsair parts and logistics within the carrier fleet. VF-12 would eventually see Corsairs operating from carriers, but it would be while operating in conjunction with the Royal Navy, who deemed the Corsair fit for duty aboard their carriers well before the US Navy.

The Royal Navy's Fleet Air Arm (FAA) flew three types of US-built carrier-based fighters during World War II. The first type acquired was the Grumman Wildcat (known as the Martlet in British service) in July 1940. In 1941, the Lend Lease Act allowed the FAA to acquire contemporary US carrier-based fighters. The FAA eventually acquired both the Vought F4U Corsair and Grumman Hellcat. Squadron Number 1830 (No 1830) completed conversion training in the US first among British units and received new F4U-1As (known as Corsair IIs). The squadron's pilots developed a method to tame the Corsair's visibility limitations while approaching a carrier. The pilot executed a gradual turn while on final approach instead of the traditional straight in approach. This allowed the pilot to see the carrier up until the last second, when the pilot would level the wings and cut the throttles once over the deck. The technique developed by the British was later emulated by both USN and USMC squadrons.

An F4U-1 from VF-17 catches a wire on board the USS *Bunker Hill* (CV-17) during a carrier landing on July 11, 1943. Pilots from VF-17 successfully completed their carrier qualifications but were ordered to operate as a land-based squadron when sent into combat. (NMNA)

Engines

Production F4U-1 Corsairs were powered by a Pratt & Whitney R-2800-8 engine, producing 2,000 horsepower at takeoff. The R-2800-8 was equipped with an auxiliary supercharger that could operate at two speeds with three different settings: neutral, low, and high. When in neutral, the R-2800-8 performed like a single-stage engine: when in high or low the intake air is compressed in two stages. The intake air is compressed by the auxiliary blower, then cooled by the intercooler. It is then sent through the main stage blower before entering the cylinders. Neutral is used for low altitudes, low gear for medium altitudes, and high gear for high altitudes. The engine's power was transmitted through the use of a 13-foot 4-inch diameter three-bladed constant-speed Hamilton-Standard Hydromatic propeller.

Late-model F4U-1As were fitted with an R-2800-8W (W designating water injection) powerplant that introduced water injection for an additional burst of power for a limited time. Known as war emergency power, or WEP, this innovation was devised by Pratt & Whitney for the Army Air Force's Republic P-47 Thunderbolt to give the large fighter additional power in a dogfight. With multiple Navy and Marine aircraft utilizing the R-2800 as a powerplant, it was easy to see how the Navy became interested. The water injection system allowed for higher manifold pressures, permitting the engine to reach 2,700rpm. Engaging the water injection system was simple: a small safety wire stopped the throttle handle from advancing completely (or the last ⅜ of an inch). In an emergency, the pilot just advanced the throttle handle completely to full open, breaking the wire and engaging the system. When the throttle was in any other position other than full throttle, the system would automatically turn off. A green warning light in the cockpit would flash after two minutes and remain on while the throttle was in the full open position. This feature was first incorporated on late production F4U-1s.

Operational Corsair Powerplants				
Pratt & Whitney Powerplant	Horsepower at takeoff & RPM	Aircraft	Blades	Hamilton Standard Propeller # and size
R-2800-8	2,000/2,700	F4U-1/F4U-2/FG-1/F3A-1/	(3)	#6501/6443 size 13ft,4in
R-2800-8W		F4U-1A/F4U-1D/F4U-1C	(3)	#6501A-0 size 13ft,1in
R-2800-18W	2,100/2,800	F4U-4/F4U-4B/F4U-4P/F4U-7	(4)	#6501A-0 size 13ft,2in
R-2800-42W	2,100/2,800	F4U-4/F4U-4B	(4)	#6501A-0 size 13ft,2in
R-2800-32W	2,300/2,800	F4U-5/F4U-5N/F4U-5NL/F4U-5P	(4)	#6637A-0 size 13ft,2in
R-2800-83WA	2,300/2,800	AU-1	(4)	#6837A-0 size 13ft,2in

Propeller

All three United Aircraft Corporation subsidiaries, Vought-Sikorsky, Pratt & Whitney and Hamilton Standard, contributed to the success of the Corsair. Hamilton Standard's propeller design was just as important to the prototype Corsair as the XR-2800 powerplant. The prototype Corsair utilized a constant speed propeller (with three blades), meaning that as the engine built up power, the pitch of the propeller blades changed through the use of a hydraulically-operated prop governor. As the manifold pressure climbed, the angle of the propeller blades would increase to allow the propeller to remain at a constant rpm and operate at its greatest efficiency while decreasing drag. Hamilton Standard propellers fitted to Corsairs would evolve over time, as did the F4U. Newer designs from the company allowed for smaller propeller diameters in late model F4U-1s even though these variants saw an increase in power. The hydromatic four-blade propeller employed on the F4U-4 had a diameter of 13 feet 2 inches. The propeller fitted to the F4U-5 had thinner blade tips to deal with the new model's increased speed, and the hub design was also reinforced to deal with the change in thrust axis.

An early-production Goodyear FG-1 Corsair (BuNo 13078) assigned to VMF-323. This aircraft was involved in a landing accident in September 1943. Early Corsairs were very unforgiving, earning the aircraft the nickname "Ensign Eliminator." The aircraft's stall characteristics on approach, bounce on landing, and brute power of the R-2800 could easily overwhelm a pilot in training. (National Archives)

Fuselage/Body

The Corsair's body was made of pre-stressed aluminum panels, much of which was spot-welded onto the frame. Internal stiffeners strengthened the joints, minimizing the use of rivets that caused parasitic drag. Radial engine designs like the R-2800 incurred high drag penalties due to the engine's large cross section. In an effort to reduce drag, Beisel's team designed a streamlined fuselage that conformed behind the cowling of the R-2800. The all-metal fuselage housed the Corsair's 237-gallon self-sealing main fuel tank, a single-seat cockpit, and the radio compartment. Provisions were made for a 160-gallon drop-tank below the fuselage. Corsair cockpit layouts saw numerous changes throughout the aircraft's production life. The majority of Corsairs had no floorboards. Instead, pilots had two leg rails, providing a clear line of sight to a small bombing window at the bottom of the fuselage. This window was a holdover from the prototype, intended to aid the pilot in bombing enemy aircraft formations. Vought discarded the rails and bombing window and incorporated a standard floorboard with the F4U-4.

Wings and Undercarriage

The Corsair's most recognizable feature was its inverted gull wing design. A conventional wing design would have required tall main landing gear to give the propeller enough ground clearance. This was not acceptable for multiple reasons. The aircraft was designed as a Navy fighter, so consequently its gear needed to withstand the rigors of carrier landings. Tall gear tended to produce a large bounce during carrier landings. The main gear was situated at the wing's lowest point to keep it as short as possible. It was attached to the main beam or wing spar and retracted rearward, with the wheel struts rotating 90 degrees into a fully-enclosed wheel well in the inner wing or wing knuckles. The main gear was also designed to be used as a dive brake. A dive-brake control on the left sub instrument panel allowed the pilot to lower the main gear while keeping the tail wheel stowed. The dive brakes needed to be set prior to reaching 225 knots (due to air load limits on the extending mechanism). In the event of complete hydraulic failure, the main gear could be extended with a CO_2 system, while a spring system would lower the tail wheel.

The Corsair utilized a non-laminar flow wing, built around the NACA 2415 airfoil. This airfoil permitted sufficient lift at slow speeds (needed during carrier approaches) without hindering the aircraft's high-speed performance. The Corsair's wingspan measured 41 feet, giving the bent wing bird 314 square feet of total wing area. The wings were connected to the fuselage at 90-degree angles for smooth air flow between the fuselage and the wing surfaces. The outer wing (past the wing knuckle or inner wing) housed the Corsair's armament as well as internal wing tanks on the F4U-1. To protect the 62-gallon wing tanks from gunfire, these tanks incorporated a CO_2 vapor dilution system, making the atmosphere above the fuel inert. The F4U-1D had the internal wing tanks removed and incorporated positions for multiple external fuel tanks (two 150-gallon drop tanks on each inner wing position and one 175-gallon tank carried on the centerline). Later Corsairs would retain the dry wing for ease of maintenance. Interestingly, the Corsair's wing used a mix of materials, most of which was aluminum, although the outer wing panels were covered in fabric and the ailerons were built out of plywood covered in fabric for their protection (metal ailerons were tested, but never made it to production). The F4U-5 was the first production model to replace the fabric outer wing panels with metal panels. However, the F4U-5 still utilized fabric-covered moving surfaces.

An F4U-1D (BuNo 82332) from VMA-322 "Fighting Gamecocks" on the newly-captured Kadena Airfield, Okinawa. VMF-322 was one of three Corsair squadrons assigned to Marine Aircraft Group 33 (MAG-33) operating from Kadena Airfield in the early stages of Operation *Iceburg*. The squadron's lead element was sent ashore on April 3, 1945, where their LST (*LST 599*) was hit by a kamikaze attack, wounding several squadron members. (National Archives)

Corsairs utilized hydraulically-controlled slotted wing flaps. These were designed to aid the pilot during combat maneuvering at speeds up to 175 knots. At low speeds, with the flaps set at 20 degrees, the increase in lift decreased the aircraft's turning radius. Corsairs also incorporated what was known as a "blow up" feature. This feature ensured that the flaps would automatically retract when under excessive air loads, and once the airspeeds were reduced the flaps would automatically return to their previous setting. In case the blow-back system was inoperative, full flaps were limited to 130 knots indicated.

The Corsair exhibited normal stall warnings in most phases of flight. Prior to a stall, the pilot would experience tail buffeting and a nose-high attitude of the aircraft. It was important for a Corsair pilot to recover from a stall before the aircraft entered into a spin. According to the F4U-1 Pilot's handbook, after a few full turns of a spin the forces required to recover the aircraft become extremely difficult. The Corsair's spin characteristics were such that pilots were not permitted to intentionally spin a F4U-1. Technical Order 30-44, *Model F4U-1, F4U-2, FG-1, and F3A-1 Airplane, Restrictions on Maneuvering*, was published to enforce this rule. A series of spin tests proved it was possible to recover an F4U-1 after four spins in either direction in a clean configuration, and after one full spin in the landing configuration if the proper actions were taken. Engineers incorporated a stall-warning light atop the main instrument panel. This gave the pilot some initial warning of an impending stall when in the landing configuration. The Corsairs had hydraulically-controlled folding wings. The wings could be folded and unfolded automatically from the cockpit when the engine was running. The wings folded vertically, giving the Corsair a height of 16 feet 1 inch in the folded position.

Internal Armament

Standard internal armament for Corsairs during World War II featured six Browning AN/M2 light barrel .50-caliber machine guns, with three in each wing. The F4U-2 night-fighter version of the Corsair had a total of five AN/M2 .50cal machine guns, three in the port wing and two in the starboard wing. One .50cal gun was removed from the starboard wing of the F4U-2 to make room for installation of the radar's wave-guide. The pilot charged the six .50cals hydraulically from within the cockpit. Each wing-gun compartment had a combustion heater, activated from within the cockpit. Vought produced 200 F4U-1Cs that carried four AN/M2 20mm cannons. One of the drawbacks to the four 20mm cannon arrangement was that there was no provision to charge the cannons from within the cockpit. The F4U-1C was the only

B

MAIN CORSAIR WEAPONS
1. .50cal machine gun installation
2. M2 20mm cannon assembly
3. M3 (T-31) 20mm cannon assembly
4. General Purpose Bombs. The types used were the AN-M30A1 100lb bomb; AN-M57A1 250lb bomb; AN-M64A1 500lb bomb; AN-M65A1 1,000lb bomb; AN-M66A2 2,000lb bomb. Illustrated is the 500lb AN-M64A1.
5. 11.75in. Tiny Tim air-to-ground rocket
6. 5in. High Velocity Aircraft Rocket (HVAR)
7. 6.5in. Anti-Tank Aircraft Rocket (ATAR)

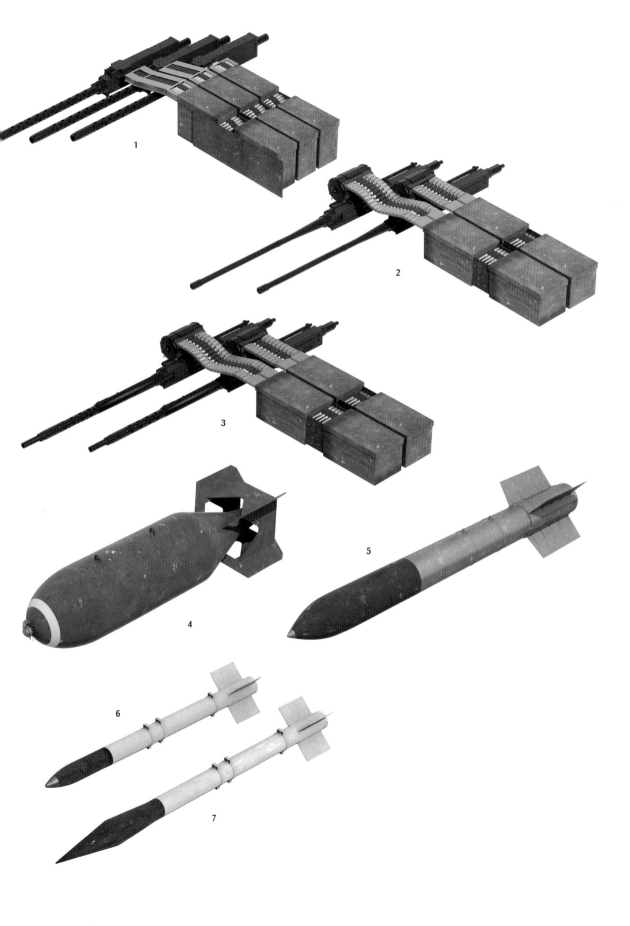

cannon version of the Corsair produced during World War II. After the war, Vought produced 297 F4U-4B Corsairs, originally designated F4U-4C, and armed with two M3 20mm cannons in each wing. The four M3 20mm cannons found on the F4U-4B became the standard armament for production F4U-5, AU-1, and F4U-7s.

Corsair X Planes				
Designation	Bureau Numbers	Qty	Model Converted	Purpose or Program
XF4U-1	1443	1	N/A	F4U Corsair Prototype
XF4U-2	02153	1	(F4U-1)	Night-Fighter Conversion
XF4U-3	17516, 49664, 02157	3	(F4U-1)	High-Altitude Interceptor
XF4U-1C	50277	1	(F4U-1)	Cannon-Equipped
F4U-4X	49763, 50301	2	(F4U-1)	F4U-4 Prototype
XF4U-4	80759 thru 80763	5	N/A	First five production F4U-4 aircraft
XF4U-5	97296, 97364, 97415	3	F4U-4	F4U-5 Prototype
XF4U-6	124665	1	F4U-5N	AU-1 Prototype
XF2G-1	13471, 13472, 14691 thru 14695	7	FG-1	F2G Prototype

TECHNICAL SPECIFICATIONS

Production Models and Operational Conversions

F4U-1

The first production F4U-1 Corsair (BuNo 02153) was flown on June 25, 1942. It was powered by a Pratt & Whitney R-2800-8 engine with a two-stage, two-speed supercharger. This gave the production model a top speed of 415mph in level flight. The F4U-1 cockpit layout was spacious in comparison to other Navy fighters. The lack of a floorboard contributed to the perception of open space. The early model proved to have several problems, however. The low seat position and framed (birdcage) canopy restricted the pilot's view. In response, engineers modified the canopy on the second production run, installing a small bubble window atop the birdcage for the purpose of relocating a rearview mirror. Second, hydraulic fluid from the cowl flap actuators and engine oil splattered the windscreen. Vought service bulletin No. 155 resolved this problem by changing the cowl flap mechanisms from hydraulic to mechanically operated. The service order also batted down the top three cowl flaps. Next, the F4U-1 revealed a tendency to bounce due to the rigid landing gear oleos. Finally, and most significantly, the F4U-1 Corsairs exhibited poor stall characteristics at approach speeds. Abruptly adding full throttle to correct the stall could lead to a worse situation known as a torque roll (inverting the aircraft due to the thrust of the engine). An unusual and inexpensive fix became apparent when the first production F4U-1(BuNo 02153) underwent conversion to the XF4U-2 night-fighter model. The aircraft was fitted with a mock radome on the right wing, and during testing pilots noticed a much more pronounced stall warning on approach than with the standard F4U-1. This would lead to incorporating a small spoiler on later models. To help pilots avoid the stall at approach speeds while flying the F4U-1, a stall warning light was installed in F4U-1 cockpits.

Major Gregory J. Weissenberger, the commanding officer of VMF-213 "The Hellhawks," is seen climbing into his F4U-1 to lead another mission from Guadalcanal. His Corsair (BuNo 02288) was started by ground personnel. (NMNA)

F4U-1 Production	
Total Built	2,814
F4U-1	733
F4U-1A	2,081
Bureau Numbers	
F4U-1	02153 through 02736
	03802 through 03841
	17392 through 17455
	18122 through 18166
F4U-1A (late production)	17456 through 18121
	18167 through 18191
	49660 through 50349
	55784 through 56483

FG-1 and F3A-1

Vought expanded its factory in Stafford, but the factory's production capacity could not fulfill the Navy's requirement for F4U-1s. The US Navy contracted two companies to co-produce Corsairs to increase production numbers. The first was Brewster Aeronautical Corporation. Brewster had built the first monoplane fighter delivered to the US Navy, the F2A Brewster Buffalo. The Navy awarded Brewster a contract to license-build Corsairs on November 1, 1941. Unfortunately, the company struggled to produce aircraft due to mismanagement and labor issues. The problems continued to a point where the company defaulted on other contracts. The Navy took delivery of the first F3A-1 Corsair (BuNo 04515) in March 1943. Brewster produced 735 examples of the F3A-1 from their Johnsville, Pennsylvania plant before going out of business in 1944.

The second company, Goodyear Aircraft Corporation, received approval to license-build Corsairs in December 1941. The first Goodyear Corsair (designated FG-1 BuNo 12992) was test flown on February 25, 1943 and delivered to the Navy the same month. Although Goodyear was the second company selected, it was the first to produce a license-built version of the Corsair. This occurred nearly a month before Brewster. Goodyear built 377 Corsairs in their Akron, Ohio plant in 1943 alone.

A number of FG-1s were built with non-folding wings in order to improve performance by reducing the aircraft's weight with the added benefit of minimizing complexity. Two separate methods were used to create the fixed wing FG-1s. The first and easiest method was to not install the wing-folding mechanisms while the FG-1s were on the production line. The second option was to remove the folding mechanisms in the field using a kit. This could be done for Vought and Brewster Corsairs as well, but was a bit more difficult. On Dec 6, 1943, the Bureau of Aeronautics issued guidance on weight-reduction measures for the F4U-1, FG-1, and F3A. Corsair squadrons operating from land bases were authorized to remove catapult hooks, arresting hook, and associated equipment, which eliminated 48 pounds of unnecessary weight. Some of the parts were turned back into the supply system for other units, while others would be stored as loose equipment and could later be reinstalled.

FG-1 and F3A-1 Production	
Goodyear-built	2,010
Brewster-built	735
Bureau Numbers	
FG-1	12992 through 14685
	76139 through 76148
F3A-1	04515 through 04774
	08550 through 08797
	11067 through 11293

This F4U-1A known as "Ole' 122" by members of VMF-111 holds a unique place in World War II aviation history as it is the only aircraft known to have received an official citation during the war. Operating from the Gilbert and Marshall Islands, the aircraft set a record for reliability. The F4U-1A flew 100 missions without turning back for mechanical problems, constituting 400 flight hours and over 80,000 miles on the same engine. (National Archives)

F4U-1A (Unofficial Designation)

The F4U-1A designation emerged as an unofficial designation used to distinguish late-production F4U-1 aircraft that incorporated major design changes from the original F4U-1. Changes included the installation of a 6-inch stall strip on the outer starboard wing, which improved the asymmetrical stall characteristics. A fix to the Corsair's oleo strut issues reduced the aircraft's bounce on landing. The Corsair's poor visibility while taxiing also received due attention. Vought engineers lengthened the tail-wheel strut and installed an adjustable seat for better forward visibility. The F4U-1A incorporated a wider blown-glass canopy with two reinforcing bars and a simplified windscreen instead of the birdcage canopy and rear-view windows. Additional cockpit improvements included a new instrument panel, armored headrest, lengthened control stick, improved rudder/brake pedals, and a new gun sight. The first Corsair to receive the modifications was BuNo 02557, which was used as a test bed. The first production aircraft

incorporating the improvement was BuNo 17647. The F4U-1A's range was also increased with the ability to carry a single centerline drop tank, or a centerline bomb rack, starting with BuNo 17930.

Late-production run F4U-1As received a new version of the Pratt & Whitney Double Wasp engine, the R-2800-8W. This engine had the capability to utilize water injection in an emergency, thereby increasing horsepower by 250hp for five minutes. The first F4U-1A powered by an R-2800-8W with water injection was BuNo 55910. All subsequent F4U-1As received the new engine. Goodyear Corsairs, along with their Brewster siblings, received the new powerplant starting with FG-1 (BuNo 13992) and F3A-1 (BuNo 11208).

Clipped Wing Corsairs

Vought designated Corsairs destined for the Royal Navy's Fleet Air Arm (FAA) as F4U-1Bs. Goodyear and Brewster built Corsairs as FG-1B and F3A-1B respectively. The first Corsairs supplied to the Royal Navy were Vought-built F4U-1s. These aircraft, delivered in May 1943, were given the designation of Corsair I by the British Air Commission. Both maintainers and pilots from the FAA converted to the Corsair at Quonset Point Naval Air Station, Rhode Island. The FAA's experience with adapting former Royal Air Force aircraft for carrier operations eased their efforts in making the Corsair fit for carriers. One issue that affected its use aboard RN carriers was the Corsair's wing-folding mechanism. The Corsair's wings folded vertically above the cockpit, giving the aircraft a stowed height of 16 feet 1 inch. British carrier hangar decks had exactly 16 feet of height clearance (due to Royal Navy carriers having armored flight decks, a feature that would be invaluable during the latter stages of World War II). The British replaced the standard wing tips from the Corsair with wooden fillets. The fillet would be placed on wing station 149. By placing the fillet on an already established wing station, the modification had little impact on an already busy production line. The wing modification reduced the length of each wing by 8 inches, thereby giving the British Corsairs better roll rates. The first Corsair to be delivered with the clipped wing modification was Brewster-built BuNo 17952, known as the Corsair III in British service. Of the 735 Brewster Corsairs built, 430 found their way into the Royal Navy inventory. The 94 F4U-1 Corsairs built by Vought for British use were retrofitted with the clipped wing modification.

F4U-1D / FG-1D

The F4U-1D was purposely built as a fighter-bomber from the factory. It kept the F4U-1A's original armament of six .50cal machine guns, and offered new provisions to carry up to eight unguided rockets on the outer wings (four on each wing) and two pylons for either napalm, 1,000lb bombs, or drop tanks on the wing knuckles. It also retained a centerline pylon (for drop tanks or bombs). The aircraft was powered by an R2800-8W Double Wasp engine. Unlike the F4U-1C, which was only produced by Vought, the F4U-1D model was built by Goodyear as well, designated as the FG-1D. The F4U-1D models saw service before their cannon-equipped sibling, the F4U-1C. During the production run, the F4U-1D was eventually fitted with a smaller diameter propeller (of 13 feet 1 inch instead of the standard 13 feet 4 inch propeller), starting with BuNo 57356. Another production-line modification was the addition of a cutout step in the starboard flap, allowing easier access for the pilot.

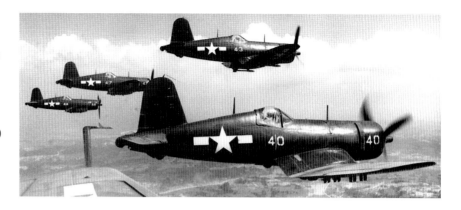

A mix of FG-1D and F4U-1D Corsairs from VMF-323, the "Death Rattlers," seen after delivering napalm and rockets on Kushi Dake ridge, June 10, 1945. The ridge in central Okinawa served as a strong point in the Japanese defensive. (Note: the leading aircraft has two hung rockets.) (National Archives)

The first ten F4U-1Ds off the production line, starting with BuNo 50350 (FAA serial JT-555), were delivered to the Fleet Air Arm. The first F4U-1D delivered to the Navy was BuNo 50360, which has been mistakenly reported as the first production F4U-1D in some accounts. The first D model entered Navy inventory on April 22, 1944. This version saw combat in the Marshall Islands through the end of the war. The Royal New Zealand Air Force fielded 45 FG-1Ds as well.

F4U-1D / FG-1D (C Models included)	
Built	1,685/1,997
Bureau Numbers	
F4U-1D/C	50350 through 50659
	57084 through 57983
	82178 through 82852
FG-1D	67055 through 67099
	76149 through 76739
	87788 through 88453
	92007 through 92701

F4U-1C

Early on, Vought experimented with upgrading the Corsair's armament from six .50cal machine guns to four 20mm cannons. The first cannon-equipped prototype (BuNo 50277), designated the XF4U-1C, flew in August 1943. Vought produced 200 cannon-equipped Corsairs from the F4U-1D production line. The F4U-1C featured four AN-M2 20mm cannons (two in each wing), with a total of 924 rounds. The cannons were based on the Hispano-Suiza .404. Additionally, the C model had two pylons on each wing, capable of carrying up to four 5-inch rockets in total.

VMF-311 was the first Marine squadron to put the new cannon-equipped F4U-1C into combat. On January 6, 1945, 19 F4U-1Cs from the squadron bombed and strafed Wotje Atoll in the Marshall Islands. Three Marine squadrons (VMF-311, VMF-441, and VMF-314) and two Navy squadrons, VF-84 and VF-85, operated the F4U-1C during Operation *Iceberg*, the battle for Okinawa. The F4U-1C was met with mixed reviews from the pilots. The M2 cannons could not be recharged from inside the cockpit and they had a slow rate of fire, making them difficult to use in aerial engagements. On the other hand, the F4U-1C's cannons were extremely effective against ground targets, using a mix of standard and armor-piercing shells. The F4U-1C model paved the way for later cannon versions of the Corsair after the war.

This F4U-1C, assigned to VMF-311 "Hells Belles," was photographed at Yontan Airfield during the battle of Okinawa, April 1945. The squadron's first air-to-air kill took place over Okinawa on April 7, 1945. The F4U-1C was the only cannon variant of the Corsair used during World War II. (National Museum of the Marine Corps)

F4U-1P

A handful of F4U-1D Corsairs were converted to serve as photo-reconnaissance aircraft during the later stages of the war; these aircraft would serve operationally in both the USMC and USN. The Navy had an interest in converting 60 Corsairs for the photo-reconnaissance role prior to the initial production of the F4U-1. Vought provided the US Navy with drawings and a mockup of the camera installation. The Navy converted the aircraft itself in order not to disrupt Vought's production line. The aircraft designated as F4U-1P utilized a remotely-controlled camera installed in the lower rear-section of the fuselage with a single ventral window. The camera mount carried a single camera; however, the mount could accommodate various types of aerial cameras to include the K-17, K-18, K-21, and F-56.

F4U-1C Production	
Built	200
Bureau Numbers	57657 through 57659
	57777 through 57791
	57966 through 57983
	82178 through 82189
	82260 through 82289
	82370 through 82394
	82435 through 82459
	82540 through 82582
	82633 through 82639
	82740 through 82761

F4U-2 Night Fighter

The United States Navy Bureau of Aeronautics forwarded a proposal for a night-fighter version of the Corsair to the Vought-Sikorsky Aircraft Division on November 8, 1941. Vought, in conjunction with the Massachusetts Institute of Technology and the Sperry Gyroscope Company, proceeded with the project to create a night fighter out of the Corsair. Vought laid the foundation for the aircraft by building a full-scale mockup. Vought foresaw delays with producing the new model as the company was hard pressed with the production of the F4U-1 and had a crowded engineering department. The Bureau of Aeronautics remained undeterred and instituted a plan to have the Naval Aircraft Factory (NAF) in Philadelphia, Pennsylvania build the night-fighter version of the Corsair. The NAF would eventually modify 32 Corsairs from the F4U-1 production line, including the first production

One of only two field-modified F4U-2s is seen taking off from the deck of the USS *Windham Bay* (CV-92). VMF(N)-532 converted two F4U-1As into night fighters in the field at Roi Island. (NMNA)

Corsair (BuNo: 02153). The modification program was named Project Roger. Vought, in full cooperation with the Navy, supplied NAF with preliminary sketches of the wing, instrument panel, and radio compartment modifications needed to create the F4U-2. Subsequently, Squadron VMF (N)-532 modified two additional Corsairs into night fighters in the field. At least one fleet-modified F4U-2 utilized a late-production F4U-1s airframe with a bubble canopy.

The most noticeable external difference between the F4U-1 and the F4U-2 was the airborne interception radar, mounted in a radome on the starboard wing's leading edge. The standard armament of three M2 machine guns per wing was reduced to two on the starboard side of the F4U-2 to accommodate the wave-guide. To power the radar, a 60-amp generator was installed. A small air scoop located on the starboard side of the fuselage cooled the generator. Exhaust dampeners were utilized to conceal the engine's exhaust at night. The standard Corsair high-frequency radio was replaced in favor of VHF radio, with a whip antenna atop the fuselage behind the cockpit. A second whip antenna was installed below the fuselage for use with an Identify Friend or Foe (IFF) system. The antenna was located aft of the bombing window. The F4U-2 had a radio altimeter with two additional antennas located on the aircraft's belly for night carrier landings. Internal changes were numerous, and included a new instrument panel, instrumentation lighting, radar-controlled sights, and an IFF radar beacon. Both an autopilot/maneuvering pilot were also tested.

A detachment of F4U-2 Corsair night fighters from VF(N)-101 prepare to launch from the USS *Enterprise* (CV-6) for a raid against Truk, February 1944. The detachment operated from the USS *Enterprise* from Jan–July 1944 and was credited with destroying five enemy aircraft, with two probables. (National Archives)

The first F4U-2 (which happened also to be the first production F4U-1) took to the skies in its modified form on January 7, 1943. On October 31, 1943 an F4U-2 pilot from VF(N)-75, Lt Hugh D. O'Neill, Jr was credited with the first successful (ground-vectored) night interception of the Pacific War, shooting down a Japanese Betty bomber. Three squadrons eventually flew the night-fighter version of the Corsair in combat during the course of the World War II, VF(N)-75, VF(N)-101 and VMF(N)-532.

F4U-2 Production	
Naval Aircraft Factory/ Conversions	32
Fleet Conversions	2
Total	34
Bureau Numbers	
F4U-1 Conversions	02153, 02243, 02421, 02432, 02434, 02436, 02441, 02534, 02617, 02622, 02624, 02627, 02632, 02641, 02672, 02673, 02677, 02681, 02682, 02688, 02692, 02708, 02709, 02710, 02731, 02733, 03811, 03814, 03816, 17412, 17418, 17423
F4U-2 Fleet Conversions	17473, 02665

F2G Super Corsairs (Wasp Major)

A program to combine Pratt & Whitney's most powerful radial engine, the R-4360 Wasp Major, with the Corsair began in March of 1943. Vought loaned a single F4U-1 (BuNo 02460) to Pratt & Whitney for use as a test bed. The Navy decided to have Goodyear develop the combination further in order to keep production at Vought running smoothly. Goodyear designated the new aircraft as the F2G. Goodyear planned to build two separate versions, one for land-based operations and one for carrier operations. The land-based version, designated F2G-1, still incorporated folding wings, which could only be folded manually. The F2G-2, built for carrier operations, had both hydraulically-operated folding wings and arresting gear. There were armament differences between the two variants as well. The F2G-1 was armed with four .50cal machine guns while the carrier-based version had six.

One of only two F2G-1s left in existence, this aircraft (BuNo 88458) finished third in a trio of Super Corsairs that won the 1949 Thompson Trophy. The aircraft was restored in its original racing colors by owner Bob Odegaard. Mr Odegaard was later killed in an accident involving an F2G-1 (BuNo 88463) on September 7, 2012. (Pima Air & Space Museum Collection)

Several Corsairs coming off the Goodyear assembly line supported the test program. Seven preproduction aircraft were utilized as test beds and given XF2G designations. External differences between the F2G and standard production Corsairs were apparent. First, the F2G series utilized a bubble canopy (similar to the Republic P-47D Thunderbolt and the North American P-51D Mustang). Second, the aircraft's vertical stabilizer was a foot taller than the standard Corsair and incorporated a split rudder. Third, the R-4360 Wasp Major engine extended the nose and had the air scoop situated on top of the cowling toward the back of the engine. Only ten were built (five F2G-1s and another five F2G-2s) due to the cancellation of the program. Many of the Super Corsairs would end up in private hands, finding new careers as pylon racers. The most notable race results came in 1947 and 1949. Cook Cleland flew an F2G-2 Super Corsair BuNo 88463 to win the Thompson Trophy in 1947. The 1949 Thompson Trophy race saw all three podium positions taken by F2G Corsair pilots, with Cleland taking first for a second time.

F2G Production	
Production	10 built
Bureau Numbers	
F2G-1	88454 through 88458
F2G-2	88459 through 88463

XF4U-3 and FG-3

Vought was awarded a contract to convert three F4U Corsairs into high-altitude interceptors. The Corsairs were to be fitted with Pratt & Whitney XR-2800-16 engines, a four-bladed Hamilton Standard propeller, and a Birmann type turbo-supercharger. The four-bladed propeller and air-intake scoop utilized for the turbo-supercharger (situated centerline past the engine cowling) made the XF4U-3 easily distinguishable from other Corsairs. The first flight of the XF4U-3A took place on March 26, 1944, and the aircraft in question was a converted F4U-1 BuNo 17516. The second prototype (designated XF4U-3B) converted from an F4U-1A (BuNo 49664) was powered by an R-2800-14W engine due to delays at Pratt & Whitney with the R-2800-16 engine. During testing the XF4U-3 showed promise, as the aircraft attained 480mph at 40,000 feet. A third Corsair BuNo 02157 was selected for the program, but crashed shortly after being converted. The Navy wanted to limit Vought's involvement with the project in order for the company to concentrate on the new F4U-4 production for the war effort. The conversion project would be given to the Naval Aircraft Modification Unit (NAMU) located in Johnsville, PA. NAMU converted 27 FG-1D aircraft into turbo-supercharged Corsairs designated FG-3s. The last FG-3 was struck from the United States Navy's inventory in 1949.

FG-3 Production	
Production	27 converted from FG-1D
Bureau Numbers	
FG-3	76450, 76708, 92252, 92253, 92283, 92284, 92300, 92328, 92232, 92338, 92341, 92344, 92345, 92354, 92359, 92361, 92363, 92364, 92367, 92369, 92382 through 92385, 92429, 92430, 92440

F4U-4

The F4U-4 represented the first major production change at Vought. Prior to this, the F4U-1 had been effectively upgraded through a system of master changes. One of the identifying features on the new Corsair was a four-bladed Hamilton-Standard propeller with a diameter of 13ft 1in. Early model F4U-4s were powered by the new "C" series Pratt & Whitney R-2800-18W (water-injected) engine, featuring forged cylinder heads. Some late model F4U-4s used the R-2800-42W. The original powerplant (R-2800-18W) produced 2,100 horsepower at takeoff. The engine produced more horsepower at takeoff and at critical altitudes than the older R-2800-8 or "B" series engines. The water injection system was essentially the same, with a notable difference being the inclusion of a thumb latch on the throttle instead of the earlier safety wire. The engine used an electric starter without a cartridge breech. Covering the powerplant was a redesigned cowling featuring a new auxiliary-stage air-duct entrance (or chin scoop) at the bottom of the nose cowl. The cowl flaps were redesigned to be larger and fewer in number. As a result, the F4U-4 possessed five cowl flaps on each side instead of the 15 found on F4U-1s.

The fuel system differed significantly from past Corsairs. The F4U-4 had one main self-sealing fuel cell of 230 gallons (7 gallons less than the F4U-1). As with late model F4U-1s, Vought eliminated the wing tanks, giving the F4U-4 a dry wing. However, the new Corsair also had provisions to carry two drop tanks, one on each inner wing pylon. No provisions were made for a centerline drop tank, nor was there a reserve for the main tank. A warning light indicated when 50 gallons remained in the tank.

The F4U-4 had a completely redesigned cockpit, featuring a more efficient instrument panel that reduced the pilot's workload. A shortened control stick, simplified controls on both the right and left shelves set in a reclined position, and revised rudder pedals for maximum pilot comfort were introduced. The new cockpit was designed with pilot comfort in mind and included a cigar lighter, a new armored seat with armrests, and for the first time, a floorboard instead of foot rails (also known as foot troughs). The addition of a floorboard had multiple benefits, as it prevented objects from

An F4U-4 (BuNo 81066) of VMF-212 taxies on Kadena Airfield, Okinawa, in preparation for a close air support mission. Marine Aircraft Group-14 (MAG-14) received new F4U-4 Corsairs during the closing stages of World War II. VMF-212 was the first Marine squadron to operate the F4U-4 in combat. (National Archives)

falling out of reach and reduced the chance of a hydraulic leak entering the cockpit. Additional armor protection was added as well as a flat bullet-proof windscreen. The new Corsair came with a blown canopy (with no reinforcement bars) for better visibility, carried over from late model F4U-1Ds. Vought replaced the bombing window with an access door large enough for maintenance personnel to enter. Cockpit access from outside the aircraft was also made easier with the addition of a fuselage step, cowl panel grip and a flap step.

The XF4U-4 prototype made its first flight on April 19, 1944. The new Corsair posted a top speed of 446mph in level flight. The first Marine Aircraft Group to receive the F4U-4 was MAG-14 in May 1945. The group familiarized themselves with the new model in the Philippines campaign before moving to Okinawa during the latter stages of Operation *Iceberg*. The production run of the F4U-4 ended in 1947, with a total of 2,357 built. The production run included three subvariants based on the F4U-4, two of which would see frontline service. These included 297 F4U-4Bs (armed with four M3 20mm cannons (two in each wing), and nine photo-reconnaissance versions (designated F4U-4P). Two F4U-4s (BuNo 97361 and 80764) were converted as night fighters and designated F4U-4Ns. These aircraft armed with the standard six .50cal machine guns were used as test-beds for later night-fighter variants of the Corsair.

F4U-4 Production	
Production	2,357 built
Bureau Numbers (all variants included)	62915 through 63071 80764 through 82177 96752 through 97531

F4U-4B

The F4U-4B armament differed from the standard F4U-4. The standard F4U-4 used six .50cal machine guns (three in each wing), while the F4U-4B version utilized four M3 (T-31) cannons (two in each wing). The new M3 cannons were far superior to those used by the first cannon-equipped F4U-1C during World War II. Other armament differences included the use of Mk9 rocket launchers (capable of carrying four rockets or bombs per wing). Damage occurred to the flaps during the initial rocket-firing trials, so in order to remedy this the first two launchers on each side closest to the inner wing were staggered. Several unofficial sources over the years have claimed that the F4U-4B served in combat during World War II, but this would seem unlikely as the accelerated service tests of the armament installation for F4U-4Bs took place in June through December of 1946. According to US Navy aircraft history cards, the cannon-equipped F4U-4Bs saw Navy squadron service in 1946, followed by Marine squadrons in 1947. Vought produced 297 cannon-equipped F4U-4Bs, many of which would see action with the Navy and Marine Corps during the Korean War. All operational Corsair variants following the F4U-4B were armed with the M3 cannons.

C **F4U-4, BuNo 82050, VF-32 , THOMAS J. HUDNER JR, DECEMBER 1950**
This is the Corsair flown by Lt (JG) Hudner, USMC. Hudner was awarded the Medal of Honor for his attempt to rescue his crashed squadronmate Jessie L.Brown, who was shot down behind enemy lines in Korea.

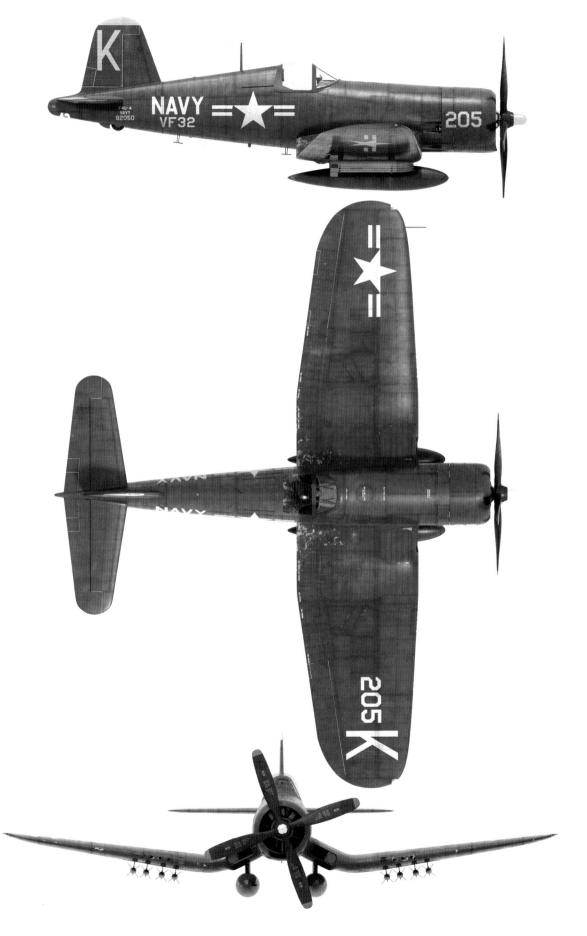

F4U-4P

Eleven of the F4U-4Bs were later converted into photo-reconnaissance aircraft. These aircraft were fitted with a single K-18 aerial camera with a 24-inch focal length. The camera was positioned aft of the cockpit on a pivot point, allowing the pilot to take photographs from three positions from within the aircraft's fuselage: one port oblique camera window, one starboard oblique camera window, and one vertical camera window located at the bottom. The K-18 aerial camera had both manual and automatic control settings utilizing an intervalometer. A camera control panel was placed on the starboard console of the cockpit. The K-18's camera was originally designed for vertical shots, but the camera was capable of taking low-altitude oblique shots as well. The F4U-4Ps retained their M3 20mm cannons for defensive purposes. This allowed the photo model Corsairs to participate in strikes prior to conducting their photo runs for battle-damage assessments.

Ordnancemen aboard the USS *Philippine Sea* (CV-47) load a AN-M64A 500lb high-explosive general-purpose bomb on to a F4U-4B prior to a strike against targets in North Korea, September 5, 1950. (National Archives)

F4U-5

On February 6, 1946, Vought received a contract from the United States Navy to build a new variant of the Corsair, designated the F4U-5. The new aircraft was powered by a Pratt & Whitney R-2800-32W with an automatic variable two-speed supercharger and water injection system. This engine was capable of producing 2,300 horsepower at takeoff. Two F4U-4 Corsairs and one cannon-equipped F4U-4B (BuNo 97296, 97364, and 97415) were later converted as prototypes. The first prototype, BuNo 97296, flew on July 3, 1946. However, the aircraft experienced an engine failure a few days later, killing Vought test pilot Dick Burroughs. The F4U-5 incorporated a mass of automated controls, including blower controls, cowl, oil cooler, and intercooler flaps. Vought redesigned the engine cowling for better efficiency. Two air inlets were positioned at four and eight o'clock on the lower cowling, thereby increasing the air flow to the twin blowers. The engine section was approximately 10 inches longer than the F4U-4 and mounted down thrust. The forward shift in the center of gravity gave the F4U-5 better longitudinal stability over the F4U-4. The longer nose did not impede the pilot's vision since the F4U-5's nose tilted three degrees down, improving forward visibility.

The F4U-5 was the first Corsair model to have all-metal outer wing panels. The variant featured a fully enclosed tail wheel and arrestor hook, reducing aerodynamic drag. The empennage of the F4U-5 utilized spring tabs on the rudder and elevator, making the Corsair easier to handle. Fabric was still used to cover the elevator and rudder and to protect the plywood ailerons. The F4U-5 had its cockpit updated to lessen the workload of the pilot, featuring a newly-designed seat with armrests, increased leg room, a heated cockpit, and even a cigarette lighter with ashtray. The oxygen system was changed to a console-mounted configuration. The ability to jettison the canopy in previous models was replaced in favor of a compressed air canopy emergency opening system. Additionally, Vought introduced a large access door on the starboard side behind the cockpit to improve access for maintenance procedures.

Pilot access was also improved with the addition of a telescopic step on the starboard side. Vought designed the step to extend and retract with the tail wheel. The arresting hook was also interconnected to the tail wheel, using a mechanical latching device over the hydraulic system used in previous models. The F4U-5's fire-control system (Mark 6 Mod.0) utilized a Mark 8 gyroscopic lead computing gun sight, which could be switched for effective use for both the four M3 (T-31) 20mm cannons and rockets. Vought incorporated electric heating for the cannons and pitot tube to enable high-altitude operations.

The first production F4U-5 took off on its maiden flight on October 1, 1947. The United States Marine Corps and US Navy received their first deliveries of F4U-5s in 1948. The F4U-5's automation was met with mixed reviews from the fleet. However, the aircraft's improved performance was much appreciated. The F4U-5 was the fastest Corsair produced in quantity, with a maximum speed of 470mph, a maximum rate of climb of 3,780 feet per minute, and a service ceiling of 41,400 feet.

F4U-5 Production	
Production	223 built
Bureau Numbers	121793 through 122066
	122153 through 122206
	123144 through 123203
	124441 through 124560
	124665 through 124724

F4U-5N

The F4U-5N was a night-fighter version of the F4U-5. It incorporated an X-band search and intercept (AN/APS-19 and 19A) radar. The scanner and receiver transmitter were stationed on the starboard wing, similar to the original Corsair night fighter, the F4U-2. The F4U-5N was equipped with an Eclipse-Pioneer P-1 automatic pilot. Located on the right-hand console or shelf, the autopilot could be overridden by the pilot through manipulation of the aircraft's standard controls. Vought also added an AN/APN-1 radio altimeter with an adjustable radar scope in the center of the instrument panel. This circular radar scope displayed blips to represent potential contacts. The AN/APS-19A radar had four modes: intercept, aim, search, and beacon. The intercept mode could detect an aircraft within 20 miles. Once within 1,500 yards of an enemy aircraft, the radar's aim mode would provide the pilot with a firing solution. The radar could also discern IFF data for the pilot. The search mode could detect surface targets from up to 100 miles away, while the beacon mode could assist in navigation.

External differences from the F4U-5 included a streamlined radar pod mounted on the starboard wing, and metal flame dampeners to conceal engine exhaust. The armament was the standard F4U-5 configuration of four

This F4U-5N assigned to VMF(N)-513 "The Flying Nightmares" is loaded with napalm and a variety of high-explosive general-purpose bombs at Pusan West (K-1) South Korea, 1951. VMF(N)-513 was the first Marine squadron to operate from land bases within South Korea during the war. The squadron played a pivotal role during the battle for the Pusan perimeter. (NMNA)

M3 cannons. However, the gun sight was changed to a Mark 20 illuminated sight. For night-fighter gunnery training purposes the F4U-5N had three retro-reflector devices (trihedral prisms): one on the upper surfaces of each wing tip and a third located on the tail cone. The prisms were used in conjunction with a light projector and the gun camera of the pursuing aircraft. If the reflectors (of the target aircraft) reflected back at the pilot firing, he knew he was on target. The F4U-5N first saw service in 1949, with 214 produced.

F4U-5N Production	
Production	214 built
Bureau Numbers	
Prototype	124665
Production	129318 through 129417
	133833 through 133843

F4U-5NL

The frigid operating conditions encountered during the Korean War highlighted the need for a winterized variant of the F4U-5N. The result was the F4U-5NL. This new version incorporated de-icing boots on the leading edges of the wings as well as boots for the vertical and horizontal stabilizers. Additionally, Vought added de-icing systems to the windscreen and de-icing shoes to the propeller blades. In all, Vought delivered 101 winterized Corsairs. Among these, 29 were originally F4U-5N models that were modified to the NL standard.

F4U-5NL Production	
Production	101 built
Bureau Numbers	124504 through 124522
	124524 through 124560
	124665 through 124709

CORSAIR PROFILES
1. F4U-4B, BuNo, 97503, of VF-53, USS Valley Forge, CV-45, Korea, July 1950
2. AU-1, BuNo 129417, of VMA-212, Korea, 1953
3. F4U-5N, BuNo 124453, of VC-3 Det 1, Lt Guy Pierre Bordelon, Korea, 1953
4. F4U-5N, FAH-609, of Fuerza Aerea Hondurena, Maj Fernando Soto Henriquez, Toncontin, Honduras, 1969

1

2

3

4

An F4U-5N night fighter from VC-3 detachment aboard the USS *Valley Forge* (CV-45) during the ship's second deployment to Korea in 1951. The snow-covered Corsair is loaded with four general-purpose bombs. Korea's frigid winters ultimately resulted in an improved version of the F4U-5N, the F4U-5NL, incorporating de-icing equipment. (National Archives)

F4U-5P

Another subvariant of the F4U-5 used by the Navy and Marine Corps was the photo-reconnaissance version F4U-5P. The first built was BuNo 122167, with 30 aircraft being built altogether. An external feature of the F4U-5P was a streamlined blister within the vertical stabilizer to house a compass transmitter. The F4U-5P had a similar camera layout to the F4U-4P, featuring three camera windows, positioned aft of the cockpit, with electrically closable doors. The camera was remotely controlled from the cockpit and had multiple position settings, allowing the pilot to select the direction of his approach to the objective. After the pilot selected the camera position, the camera would automatically lock and illuminate a light on the console indicating the camera was in position and the camera door was open. Three different types of cameras were compatible with the F4U-5P: the standard K-18-24 (used in the older F4U-4P), the K-17-12, and K-17-24.

The first F4U-5Ps entered squadron service in 1948. The first combat action for the type was on July 3, 1950. On that date, Marine Corps F4U-5Ps from HEDRON 1 Detachment aboard the USS *Valley Forge* took photos of the first US Navy strike of the Korean War. This battle damage assessment mission was also the first combat mission flown by Marine Corps aircraft during the war.

F4U-5P Production	
Production	30 built
Bureau Numbers	121804 and 121936
	121956 through 121957
	121977 through 121978
	122019 through 122022
	122045 through 122048
	122062 through 122065
	122167 through 122174

F4U-6/AU-1

During the Korean War, the Navy developed an interest in procuring a dedicated low-level attack variant of the Corsair for use by Marine squadrons. The harsh realities of fighting in Korea prompted the need for a Corsair with upgraded communications, additional armor protection, and an increased bomb load. The Navy contracted Chance Vought to build a version of the Corsair specifically for the close-support mission. An F4U-5N (BuNo 124665) was modified by Vought, becoming the first prototype XF4U-6. Originally designated as the F4U-6, the aircraft was later re-designated the AU-1. The A in the designation stood for attack. The AU-1 utilized a single-stage, two-speed, manually-controlled, supercharged R-2800-83WA engine for optimal low-level performance. The AU-1's engine nose cowling kept the general shape of the F4U-5. Vought, however, sealed over the auxiliary stage inlets scoops found on the F4U-5. Other visual distinctions were two large antenna masts associated with the AU-1's AN/ARC-27 radio. The AN/ARC-27 system was an Ultra High Frequency (UHF) AM radio with 1,750 frequency channels and 18 preset channels. The masts were located just aft of the cockpit atop the fuselage.

In addition to the standard F4U-5 armor, the AU-1 received armor provisions for the pilot's floor, seat, and main fuel tank. The F4U-5's vulnerable oil coolers (located in the wing air inlets) were relocated into an accessory station in the wing root. The intercooler door found on the F4U-5 served as the oil cooler door. The AU-1 featured four M3 20mm cannons, similar to the F4U-5, carrying a total of 924 rounds. Vought designed the AU-1 to carry a maximum bomb load of 8,200lb (besting the AD-1 Skyraider's maximum payload by 200lb). Each wing had positions for five Aero 14A racks capable of carrying either bombs (up to 500lb each) or rockets. During testing of the AU-1, pilots found the Aero 14A rack/launchers to be adequate for dropping bombs. However, when firing rockets, they assessed that damage could occur to the rack, ailerons, and flaps. The AU-1 was similar to the F4U-5 in having positions for external fuel tanks or bombs on the inner wing or wing knuckle. The centerline position used a Mk-51 bomb rack capable of carrying a 2,000lb bomb. Two additional Mk-51 bomb racks could be carried on each inner wing station, bearing up to 1,600lb each. Armament testing recommended reducing the number of 20mm rounds from 924 to 910.

The AU-1's powerplant produced 2,300 horsepower on takeoff, equaling that of the F4U-5. However the engine was purposely built with the low altitude regime in mind, sacrificing the high-altitude performance of earlier models for increased payload. During testing the R-2800-83WA engine would surge while operating above 20,000 feet.

Reported performance figures vary on the AU-1. Some sources deemed the AU-1 the slowest of all Corsair models produced, with a top speed of 238mph at 9,500 feet. While the 238mph figure comes directly from the standard aircraft characteristic (SAC) data, it is only correct while the aircraft is configured as a bomber. In this configuration, the AU-1 would be carrying a bomb load of 4,600lb plus a 150-gallon drop tank. The same SAC report shows a max speed of 298mph at 19,700 feet while in the attack configuration (eight HVAR and two 150-gallon drop tanks). This may help discern why primary sources like Capt Bernard W. Peterson's *Short Straw*, in which he describes the AU-1 performance with high marks, varies in comparison to multiple secondary sources.

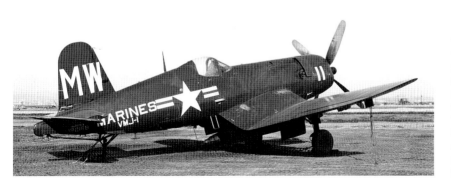

This F4U-5P Corsair (BuNo 122159) assigned to Marine Photo Reconnaissance Squadron One (VMJ-1) sits on the ramp at Pohang (K-3) South Korea, December 1952. The squadron was activated in February 1952 to consolidate all Marine photo-reconnaissance assets in theater. (National Archives)

Vought produced 111 AU-1 Corsairs. The first flight of a production AU-1 took place on January 31, 1952. In October 1952, the last AU-1 was delivered to the Marine Corps. The first squadron to take the "Able Uncle" into combat was VMA-212 "The Devil Cats." During the Korean War, two squadrons would operate the AU-1 model of the Corsair: VMA-212 and later VMA-323 "Death Rattlers."

AU-1 Production	
Production	111 built
Bureau Numbers	129318 through 129417
	133833 through 133843

F4U-7

The F4U-7 was the last model in the Corsair line. The US Navy procured 94 examples of the F4U-7 from Chance Vought's Dallas plant and supplied them to the French through the Mutual Defense Assistance Program (MDAP). The aircraft were even assigned standard US Navy bureau numbers. Following World War II, French forces found themselves fighting communist Viet Minh in an attempt to salvage their former colonial assets in the conflict known as the Indochina War. At the start of the hostilities the French Aeronavale (Naval aviation) had operated a fleet of antiquated aircraft including Douglas Dauntlesses and Supermarine Seafires. These types were later replaced by Curtiss SB2C Helldivers and F6F Hellcats. The French needed an aircraft better suited to handle close-air support missions over Indochina. The French Aeronavale was offered a range of capable aircraft to replace its aging fleet. Both the Grumman F8F Bearcat and the Hawker Sea Fury were looked at, but the French opted instead for the Corsair. The French Navy for the first time in years had procured a brand-new aircraft built exclusively to fit their current needs.

F4U-7 Production	
Production	94 built
Bureau Numbers	133652 through 133731
	133819 through 133832

An AU-1 (BuNo 129359) assigned to VMA-212 named "Miss Penny." The aircraft was named in honor of a squadron member's three-year-old daughter who was suffering from polio. Her father, 1st Lt Frank A. Nelson, went missing in action while flying a mission over North Korea. (Marine Corps Historical Division)

The first flight of the F4U-7 took place on July 2, 1952. Production ended in December of the same year. The F4U-7 combined the ruggedness and payload of the AU-1 airframe with the powerplant of the F4U-4 (utilizing an R-2800-18W engine in place of the AU-1s R-2800-83WA). Other differences included a new cowling with an air intake and duct along the bottom and a reconfiguration of the oil cooler and the installation of intercoolers. The new Corsair was a unique combination of past Corsair designs. The slanted-nose arrangement of the F4U-5 gave the French Corsair improved forward visibility, and the armament, armor and load capacity of the close-air-support focused AU-1 rounded out the F4U-7. More importantly, the French Aeronavale was supplied with plenty of spares, equipment, and tooling to support four squadrons.

Corsair Production			
Base Model	Vought	Goodyear	Brewster
F4U-1	4,699	-	-
FG-1	-	4,007	-
F3A-1	-	-	735
F4U-4	2,357	-	-
F4U-5	568	-	-
AU-1	111	-	-
F4U-7	94	-	-
Total	7,830	4,017	735
Grand Total	12,571		

Note: All sub-variant and X models are included within the base model figures, but an additional 11 Corsairs are not included (the ten limited production F2Gs and the original XF4U-1).

Corsair Specifications					
Variant	F4U-1 FG-1 F3A-1	F4U-4 FG-1D	F4U-5	AU-1	F4U-7
Powerplant Horsepower	R2800-8 2,000hp	R2800-18W 2,100hp	R2800-32W 2,300hp	R2800-83WA 2,300hp	R-2800-18W 2,100hp
Length	33ft 4in	33ft 8in	33ft 6in	34ft 1in	34ft 6in
Wingspan	41ft	41ft	41ft	41ft	41ft
Height	16ft 1in	14ft 9in	14ft 9in	14ft 10in	14ft 9in
Wing Area	314sq ft	314sq ft	314sq ft	314sq ft	314sq ft
Max Speed	417mph 19,900ft	446mph 26,200ft	470mph 26,800	438mph 9,500ft	446mph 26,200ft
Max Ceiling	36,900ft	41,500ft	41,400ft	22,000ft	41,500ft
Weight Empty Gross	8,982lb 14,000lb	9,205lb 14,670lb	9,683lb 14,106lb	9,835lb 19,400lb	9,205lb 14,670lb
Range/Miles	1,015 miles	1,005 miles	1,120 miles	N/A	1,005 miles
Internal Armament	6x .50cal	6x .50cal	4x M3 20mm	4x M3 20mm	4x M3 20mm
Ammunition	2,400	2,400	924	924	984

The first production Goodyear F2G-1 Super Corsair (BuNo 88454) is seen at the Navy Air Test Center (NATC) Naval Air Station Patuxent River Maryland, May 1947. Only ten Super Corsairs were produced. This example is on display at the Museum of Flight in Seattle, Washington. (NMNA)

Variant Summary		
Model Designations	Brief Description	Company
F4U-1	Carrier-based fighter	Vought
FG-1	Carrier-based fighter	Goodyear
F3A-1	Carrier-based fighter	Brewster
F4U-1A	Modified F4U-1 (unofficial)	Vought
F4U-1B	Company designation for FAA Corsairs	Vought
F4U-1D	Carrier-based fighter-bomber	Vought
F4U-1C	Fighter-bomber/20mm cannon	Vought
F4U-1P	Photo-reconnaissance conversion	Vought
F4U-1WM	Test aircraft, Wasp Major powerplant	Vought
FG-1D	Carrier-based fighter-bomber	Goodyear
FG-1E (proposed)	Night-fighter variant of FG-1D	Goodyear
FG-1K (proposed)	Drone variant of FG-1D	Goodyear
F4U-2	Night-fighter conversions F4U-1/1A	Vought/NAF
FG-3	FG-1D with turbo-supercharged engine	Goodyear
F4U-4	Carrier-based fighter-bomber	Vought
FG-4	Goodyear-built F4U-4 (terminated on line)	Goodyear
F2G-1	Land-based fighter (Wasp Major)	Goodyear
F2G-1D	Fighter-bomber variant of F2G-1 (Wasp Major)	Goodyear
F2G-2	Carrier-based fighter (Wasp Major)	Goodyear
F4U-4B	Carrier-based fighter-bomber/20mm cannon	Vought
F4U-4E (proposed)	Night fighter-bomber variant of F4U-4	Vought
F4U-4K (proposed)	Drone variant of F4U-4	Vought
F4U-4N	Night-fighter variant of F4U-4	Vought
F4U-4P	Photo-reconnaissance variant of F4U-4	Vought
F4U-5	Carrier-based fighter	Vought
F4U-5N	Night-fighter variant of F4U-5	Vought
F4U-5NL	Winterized night-fighter variant of F4U-5	Vought
F4U-5P	Photo-reconnaissance variant of F4U-5	Vought
F4U-6	AU-1's original designation, later changed	Vought
AU-1	Low-level attack variant	Vought
F4U-7	Fighter-bomber (French Aeronavalle)	Vought
FAA Designations		
Corsair I	Carrier-based fighter, F4U-1, standard wing	Vought
Corsair II	Carrier-based fighter, F4U-1, clipped wing	Vought
Corsair III	Carrier-based fighter, F3A-1, clipped wing	Brewster
Corsair IV	Carrier-based fighter, FG-1D, clipped wing	Goodyear

OPERATIONAL HISTORY

Guadalcanal

The first operational squadron to receive the F4U-1 Corsair was VMF-124, led by Major William E. Gise. On February 12, 1943, this squadron took the Corsair on its first combat mission. Flying from Henderson Field, Guadalcanal, VMF-124 pilots escorted a PBY Catalina on a rescue mission. On the 14th, the Marines of VMF-124 engaged their adversaries in air-to-air combat for the first time. The group was attacked by nearly 50 Zeros. The Japanese shot down all four P-38 Lightnings, which were providing top cover, and destroyed two Corsairs, including one which collided head-on with a Zero. Two PB4Ys and two P-40s were also brought down. The mission would later be known as the Saint Valentine's Day Massacre.

The pilots of VMF-124 began to realize their aircraft's advantages over the Zero in later engagements. 1st Lt Kenneth A. Walsh (a former enlisted pilot) was part of that first mission and discussed the tactics developed thereafter:

> The F4U could outperform the Zero in every aspect except slow speed maneuverability and slow speed rate of climb. Therefore, you avoided getting slow when combating the Zero. It took time, but eventually we developed tactics and employed them very effectively. When we were accustomed to the area, and knew our capabilities, there were instances when the Zero was little more than a victim.

On April 1, Walsh was credited with his first aerial victory. Corsairs from VMF-124 were flying a combat air patrol over Baroku; the CAP mission was uneventful and the F4Us were relieved by P-38s. Soon after, Zeros attacked the P-38s, unaware of the Corsairs nearby that now turned back to get into the fight. As they returned, a Zero passed directly in front of the Corsairs.

MEDAL OF HONOR CITATION, FIRST LIEUTENANT KENNETH A. WALSH, USMC

For extraordinary heroism and intrepidity above and beyond the call of duty as a pilot in Marine Fighting Squadron 124 in aerial combat against enemy Japanese forces in the Solomon Islands area. Determined to thwart the enemy's attempt to bomb Allied ground forces and shipping at Vella Lavella on August 15 1943, 1st Lt Walsh repeatedly dived his plane into an enemy formation outnumbering his own division 6 to 1 and, although his plane was hit numerous times, shot down two Japanese dive bombers and one fighter. After developing engine trouble on August 30 during a vital escort mission, 1st Lt Walsh landed his mechanically disabled plane at Munda, quickly replaced it with another, and proceeded to rejoin his flight over Kahili. Separated from his escort group when he encountered approximately 50 Japanese Zeros, he unhesitatingly attacked, striking with relentless fury in his lone battle against a powerful force. He destroyed 4 hostile fighters before cannon shellfire forced him to make a dead-stick landing off Vella Lavella where he was later picked up. His valiant leadership and his daring skill as a flier served as a source of confidence and inspiration to his fellow pilots and reflect the highest credit upon the US Naval Service.

Marine Lieutenant Kenneth A. Walsh, seen in the cockpit of an F4U-1 Corsair on Guadalcanal, 1943. Lt Walsh, a former enlisted pilot, became the first Corsair ace of the war and the first Corsair pilot to earn the Medal of Honor. Walsh ended the war with 21 kills, earning his last victory in an F4U-4 over Okinawa. (Note the rearview mirror inside the raised portion of the canopy and the tape forward of cockpit to prevent the fuel cell from leaking). (Flying Leatherneck Museum Collection)

Walsh's wingman, Lt Dean B. Raymond, splashed the Zero. Soon afterward, a second Zero was spotted above their position. Walsh got behind the unsuspecting Zero pilot and sct the enemy aircraft on fire before the Zero dived towards the sea. Walsh was credited with destroying two Zeros and a Val during the engagement. Within six months of the Corsair's introduction to combat, eight Marine fighter squadrons were operating the bent wing bird.

On May 13, 1943, Walsh brought down three more Zeros, making him the first Corsair ace; however, VMF-124 lost its commander, Major Gise, in the same action. The high-scoring Corsair pilot of the day was Captain Archie Donahue of VMF-112, who downed four aircraft. The final daylight raids over Guadalcanal took place in June 1943. On the 7th, Marines from VMF-112 destroyed seven enemy fighters at a cost of four Corsairs (all but one pilot was recovered). The last daylight raid was made on June 16, when Marine Corsair squadrons shot down a total of eight enemy aircraft while losing one of their own. The dominance of the F4U in air-to-air combat was being felt by the Japanese. On June 30, 1943, Corsairs from multiple squadrons provided cover during the New Georgia landings. Marine Corsairs claimed 58 enemy aircraft that day for the loss of three pilots and four Corsairs. VMF-121 alone accounted for 19 enemy aircraft.

Boyington & Blackburn

VMF-214 Blacksheep
Guadalcanal became home for multiple Corsair squadrons, many of which were finishing up their combat tours. This brought about a shortage of Corsair squadrons in theater, although there were plenty of F4U Corsairs and pilots awaiting assignments on Espiritu Santo in the New Hebrides. One of these

MEDAL OF HONOR CITATION, MAJOR GREGORY BOYINGTON, USMC

For extraordinary heroism and valiant devotion to duty as Commanding Officer of Marine Fighting Squadron 214 in action against enemy Japanese forces in the Central Solomons Area from September 12 1943 to January 3 1944. Consistently outnumbered throughout successive hazardous flights over heavily defended hostile territory, Major Boyington struck at the enemy with daring and courageous persistence, leading his squadron into combat with devastating results to Japanese shipping, shore installations and aerial forces. Resolute in his efforts to inflict crippling damage on the enemy, Major Boyington led a formation of 26 fighters over Kahili on October 17 and, persistently circling the airdrome where 60 hostile aircraft were grounded, boldly challenged the Japanese to send up planes. Under his brilliant command, our fighters shot down 20 enemy craft in the ensuing action without the loss of a single ship. A superb airman and determined fighter against overwhelming odds, Major Boyington personally destroyed 26 of the many Japanese planes shot down by his squadron and, by his forceful leadership, developed the combat readiness in his command which was a distinctive factor in the Allied aerial achievements in this vitally strategic area.

Major Gregory Boyington, the commanding officer of VMF-214 "Blacksheep" taxies his F4U-1A BuNo 17883 on The strip at Vella Lavella after scoring a kill on December 7, 1943. Boyington's legendary antics on the ground sometimes overshadow the fact he was a daring leader and brilliant tactician in the air. Boyington helped perfect the fighter sweep, and earned the Navy Cross and the Medal of Honor for his actions. (National Archives)

pilots was Major Gregory Boyington, a veteran combat pilot who had flown with the American Volunteer Group in China and who was anxious to get back into the fight. Due to the shortage of available Corsair squadrons, he was allowed to create an *ad hoc* squadron from the mix of combat veterans, experienced pilots, and replacement pilots waiting to be picked up. Major Boyington and his squadron of orphaned pilots were reassigned VMF-214's designation; members of VMF-214 originally wanted to name the squadron *Boyington's Bastards*, however the name *Blacksheep* was chosen, conveying the same meaning. Boyington led their first mission 14 September 14, 1943, escorting Army Air Force B-24 Liberators targeting Bougainville. Notorious for wild antics on the ground, Boyington's disdain for discipline disappeared when in the air, where he was in his natural element; he was known to have great vision, and was a decisive leader who understood and preached tactics. The squadron's 26 pilots flew combat missions for six straight weeks against Bougainville while operating mostly from Munda, New Georgia.

On their second tour, Rabaul was the target. The squadron had 38 assigned pilots and flew mostly F4U-1A models, although a few early production F4U-1 birdcage birds were still on hand. The squadron operated out of Vella Lavella, but staged missions out of multiple bases, including Empress Bay, Bougainville. The Blacksheep's commander led the first fighter sweep against Rabaul on December 17, 1943. Boyington challenged the Japanese to come up and fight by taunting them over the radio. On this mission few enemy fighters came up to fight. After this mission Boyington decreased the size of the fighter sweep formations, making them easier to manage and gaining better results. VMF-214, along with other squadrons, crippled fortress Rabaul, a hornet's nest of Japanese aerial activity. Boyington was credited with 22 air-to-air victories during his two tours as commander. The only Corsair pilot to score more aerial victories was First Lieutenant Robert M. Hanson, who was one of Boyington's Marines until later being reassigned to VMF-215. More importantly, Boyington developed effective tactics for fighter operations in theater for future use. As a squadron, VMF-214 flew over 200 combat missions, was credited with 94 air-to-air victories, and produced nine aces. During that time, it reported 12 pilots missing in action (MIA) (including Boyington, who was shot down on January 3, 1944, and spent the rest of the war as a POW) and another six wounded in combat. The squadron's operational losses amounted to one pilot injured, an admirable record for any squadron.

MEDAL OF HONOR CITATION, FIRST LIEUTENANT ROBERT M. HANSON, USMC

For conspicuous gallantry and intrepidity at the risk of his life and above and beyond the call of duty as Fighter Pilot attached to Marine Fighting Squadron 215 in action against enemy Japanese forces at Bougainville Island, November 1, 1943; and New Britain Island, January 24, 1944. Undeterred by fierce opposition, and fearless in the face of overwhelming odds, First Lieutenant Hanson fought the Japanese boldly and with daring aggressiveness. On November 1, while flying cover for our landing operations at Empress Augusta Bay, he dauntlessly attacked six enemy torpedo bombers, forcing them to jettison their bombs and destroying one Japanese plane in the action. Cut off from his division while deep in enemy territory during a high cover flight over Simpson Harbor on January 24, First Lieutenant Hanson waged a lone and gallant battle against hostile interceptors as they were orbiting to attack our bombers and, striking with devastating fury, brought down four Zeros and probably a fifth. Handling his plane superbly in both pursuit and attack measures, he was a master of individual air combat, accounting for a total of 25 Japanese aircraft in this theater of war. His personal valor and invincible fighting spirit were in keeping with the highest traditions of the United States Naval Service.

VF-17 Jolly Rogers

One of the most influential Corsair squadrons to see action during World War II was the Navy's VF-17 "The Jolly Rogers," commanded by Lieutenant Commander John T. Blackburn. Blackburn believed the Corsair was a better fighter than the Hellcat, and tried desperately to prove to the Navy that the Corsair could operate safely from a carrier. The squadron began carrier qualifications in March 1943 aboard the USS *Charger* in the Chesapeake Bay. Flying early production F4U-1s, the squadron qualified without suffering a single casualty. In July, the squadron took part in the USS *Bunker Hill*'s shakedown cruise. The squadron received new F4U-1As prior to going aboard the *Bunker Hill* in September 1943. VF-17's maintenance officer, Lt Butch Davenport, worked closely with Vought representatives to iron out most of the bugs. Many of the fixes on the modified airplanes came by way of this squadron's hard work and close cooperation with Vought.

The Navy's highest-scoring Corsair ace belonged to the famous VF-17 "Jolly Rogers squadron." Lt(JG) Ira Kepford scored 16 kills while flying with the VF-17. Here BuNo 55995 was photographed after February 19, 1944, as Kepford's last aerial victories with the squadron had already been placed on his aircraft's impressive scoreboard. (National Archives)

Blackburn received word *en route* to Pearl Harbor that his unit would operate as a land-based squadron due to logistical reasons. The squadron began combat operations from Ondonga on October 27, 1943 and later moved to Bougainville. On November 11, the squadron covered the carriers of Task Group 50.3 as they launched strikes against shipping around Rabaul. As planned, once their relief arrived, half of the formation landed aboard the USS *Bunker Hill*, while the other half landed aboard the USS *Essex*. The Corsairs re-armed, refueled, and returned to covering the Task Group before heading for home without a single loss of a Corsair while operating from the flattops. This event helped silence doubts that the Corsair could operate from carriers. VF-17 was credited with creating a tactic called "Roving High Cover," in which four to six experienced Corsair pilots would fly out ten minutes ahead of an Allied strike formation; sitting at 32,000 feet, the Corsairs would pounce on the Japanese fighters as they formed up to take on the main formation.

The Jolly Rogers had an even greater impact as the first squadron to operate the Corsair as a fighter-bomber. Utilizing field-improvised bomb racks, the squadron's first attempt to use 500lb bombs took place on February 26, 1944. Eight Corsairs led by Blackburn bombed a presumed cathouse frequented by Japanese officers on Rabaul. The mission leveled multiple structures and left the cathouse smoking. Blackburn admittedly filed a fictitious after-action report, but regardless of this, his squadron helped establish the Corsair's long and successful career as a fighter-bomber. By the end of its tour, VF-17 was credited with destroying 156 aircraft in air-to-air combat and had a dozen aces within its ranks. The squadron took pride in accounting for every aircraft it escorted and ship for which it flew cover.

Fighter-Bombers

The first Marine squadron to utilize the Corsair as a fighter-bomber was VMF-111. The Central Pacific had little in the way of air-to-air engagements, although many of the bypassed islands remained a threat to Allied aircraft as they still had vast anti-aircraft installations. The Marines of VMF-111 had created improvised bomb racks for their F4U-1s at around the same time as the Jolly Rogers. VMF-111's first bombing mission took place on March 18, 1944. Eight Corsairs took off from their base at Makin loaded with one 1,000lb bomb each for use against Japanese anti-aircraft sites on Milles Island. The Marines continued to experiment with the Corsair as a fighter-bomber and proved it could be used as a dive-bomber, making dives at up to 85-degree angles effectively and safely. When the F4U-1D fighter-bomber version of the Corsair made its debut in the Central Pacific, the ordnance loads increased exponentially. Renowned aviator Charles A. Lindbergh, a technical representative for Vought, travelled to the Pacific to study the performance of fighter aircraft under combat conditions. Lindbergh saw no better way of doing this than actually flying combat sorties. He experimented with the new F4U-1D model to see if it could carry a 4,000lb bomb load. After bombing a radio station on Wotje Atoll on September 2 with a 3,000lb bomb load, Lindbergh took off with a 2,000lb bomb loaded on the centerline rack and one 1,000lb bomb on each inner wing rack the next day. He successfully delivered the 4,000lb of bombs to an anti-aircraft site on Wotje Atoll. At the time, this was the largest bomb load carried by a single-engine fighter, equaling that of a North American B-25 Mitchell's standard bomb load. In September 1944, Corsairs from VMF-114 supported the landings on Peleilu. Corsairs from the squadron dropped napalm during close-air support missions, aiding ground forces in taking the island. Both fused and unfused napalm canisters were dropped; the unfused napalm canisters allowed Marines on the ground to ignite them with standard infantry weapons.

F4U-1A Corsairs from VMF-224 carry a single 1,000lb GP bomb each on a field-adapted centerline rack while on a strike mission against Japanese bases in the Marshalls. Multiple squadrons figured out ways to configure the F4U-1A as a fighter/bomber around the same time. As the war progressed, manufactured bomb racks replaced earlier field adaptions. After-action reports list VF-17 as the first Corsair squadron to record dropping bombs in combat in February 1944. (National Archives)

In late 1944, Marine Corsairs were relegated to neutralizing Japanese forces on bypassed islands. Admiral Halsey foresaw a better use of these assets in the Philippines and discussed his idea with General MacArthur. Squadrons from MAG-12 (VMF-115, 211, 218, and 313) were ordered to the Philippines in due course and began combat operations from Tacloban on December 5, 1944. At the start, the Corsairs were used in the fighter role and concentrated on antishipping and occasionally flying close air support. By the end of the campaign the Corsairs of MAG-12 were being used mostly for close air support missions. The Corsairs had both VHF and MHF radios, making the F4U an easy fit into the close air support role. Their first CAS mission, in support of the Army's 41st Division's landings on Basilan Island, began on March 16, 1945.

Corsairs and Carriers

In January 1944, a detachment of F4U-2s from VF(N)-101 became the first US Corsairs to operate regularly from an American aircraft carrier. The night fighters went aboard the USS *Enterprise* from January to July 1944. The Corsairs participated in both daylight raids and night-time intercept missions. By the end of their commitment, they had five confirmed kills and nearly as many probables without the loss of a single Corsair in combat. Other Marine

Capt Lee M. Quay of VMA-332 lands his F4U-4B Corsair on the deck of the USS *Bairolko* (CVE-115), completing his 100th combat mission, on July 27, 1953. On the day the armistice was signed, the squadron flew 15 combat sorties. VMA-332 received a mix of F4U-4 and F4U-4B Corsairs from VMA-312. The squadron repainted the familiar checkerboard markings on the engine cowl with red polka dots. (NMNA)

Corsair units followed as their leadership fought to place Marine squadrons aboard escort carriers (CVEs). The advent of the Japanese kamikaze tactics would hasten their arrival as two VMF squadrons were placed aboard fast carriers (CVs). The need to get Corsair fighter-bombers on carrier decks became a priority for the Navy, and ten Marine squadrons were temporarily stationed on five CVs. Another interesting project involving Marine Corsairs on carriers was Project *Crossbow*, in which Marines flying F4U-1Ds tested the new 11.75-inch Tiny Tim rocket. The F4U-1Ds were planned to be used against German V-1 sites. The plan was canceled for multiple reasons, mostly due to inter-service rivalry. Corsairs would fire the new rocket in combat in Okinawa and later in Korea.

The first Marine Corsair squadrons to operate off the CVs were VMF-124 and 213, both led by the senior squadron commander Lt Col William Millington. The squadrons boarded the USS *Essex* on December 28, 1944, and by the end of January 1945 the Marines had flown combat missions over Okinawa, Indochina, and Hong Kong. Prior to the landings on Iwo Jima, three more fast carriers joined the *Essex* (USS *Bennington*, *Bunker Hill* and *Wasp*) with two VMF Corsair squadrons assigned to each. Marine aviators flying F4U-1Ds and FG-1Ds put on an impressive display in support of the initial landings on Iwo Jima on February 19, 1945. The Corsairs conducted strafing passes starting at Suribachi and passed 200 yards ahead of the assault troops, flying above 600 feet in order to stay clear of the naval bombardment. During the fighting, Task Force 58 left Iwo Jima to conduct raids against Chichi Jima and later Honshu, taking the Marine squadrons with them.

Okinawa

On April 1, 1945, the United States Tenth Army, comprised of US Army and Marine Corps assault divisions, landed on the Hagushi beaches during Operation *Iceberg* (the invasion of Okinawa). Within a few hours, ground

E

F4U-1D, BuNo 57584, OF VMF-312, KADENA OKINAWA, 10 MAY 1945
While conducting a combat air patrol ten miles north of Kadena Airfield, Capt Kenneth L. Reusser, the division leader, observed vapor trails at 35,000 feet. Capt Reusser received permission to investigate, and his division started to climb. Two Corsairs in his formation could not climb any higher, but Capt Reusser and his wingman, 1st Lt Robert Klingman (flying F4U-1D, BuNo 57584), continued to climb. At 38,000 feet they intercepted a Kawasaki Ki-45 "Nick" and turned into it, forcing the enemy aircraft to turn north. As the Corsairs chased the Nick, they noticed it was outrunning them. Trying to give chase, they both fired off half their ammunition to lighten their aircraft. Reusser was the first to get within firing range; he fired his remaining ammo at the Nick, setting the right engine on fire and damaging the right wing. Lt Klingman attempted to fire but discovered that his guns had frozen at altitude. As the Nick continued to hold its course, Reusser stayed on the Nick's wing, distracting the Japanese pilot. Klingman decided to use his propeller to bring the aircraft down. As the Nick's gunner was firing at him, Klingman chewed off part of the rudder. Klingman would make two more passes tearing off the rudder completely as well as the right stabilizer; this caused the Ki-45 to lose control, crashing into the water. Klingman's propeller was damaged, and while losing engine power he executed a dead stick landing back at Kadena without incident. His engine and wings took hits from the Nick's gunner, and pieces of the Nick's tail-wheel were found in his Corsair's engine cowling.

forces had taken Kadena Airfield and, soon after, Yontan Airfield. On April 7, the runway on Yontan was considered ready for fighter operations, followed by Kadena on the 9th. Marine aviators relocated from the carriers to the two airfields. Corsairs based on both Kadena and Yontan airfields conducted combat air patrols to defend the Fifth Fleet from kamikaze attacks. During the Japanese defense of the Ryukyu island chain, the Imperial Japanese Navy and Army Air Force coordinated their efforts and launched a total of ten mass kamikaze attacks, known as kikusui attacks, against the Allied fleet from 5 April to 22 June, 1945. Close air support missions were primarily assigned to squadrons on the carriers (both Navy and Marine Corps). Once the kamikaze raids became less frequent, the land-based Corsairs flew CAS missions as well. Marine Corsairs were credited with destroying 436 enemy aircraft in air-to-air combat, many of which were kamikaze aircraft.

Land-Based Corsairs over Okinawa			
Squadrons	Assigned MAG & Original Airfield	Aerial Victories	Corsair Variants
VMF-224	MAG-31 Yontan	55	F4U-1D/FG-1D
VMF-311	MAG-31 Yontan	71	F4U-1C
VMF-441	MAG-31 Yontan	47	F4U-1D/C
VMF-312	MAG-33 Kadena	59.5	F4U-1D/FG-1D
VMF-322	MAG-33 Kadena	29	F4U-1D/FG-1D
VMF-323	MAG-33 Kadena	124.5	F4U-1D/FG-1D
VMF-113	MAG-22 Ie Shima	12	F4U-1D/FG-1D
VMF-314	MAG-22 Ie Shima	14	F4U-1D/C
VMF-422	MAG-22 Ie Shima	15	F4U-1D/FG-1D
VMF-212	MAG-14 Kadena	2	F4U-4
VMF-222	MAG-14 Kadena	3	F4U-4
VMF-223	MAG-14 Kadena	4	F4U-4

Royal Navy Corsairs

On December 25, 1943, the Fleet Air Arm's No. 1830 squadron landed its Corsairs aboard the HMS *Illustrious en route* to the Indian Ocean, effectively beginning sustained carrier operations for the F4U nearly nine months prior to the United States Navy. In March 1944, the HMS *Illustrious's* two Corsair squadrons, nos. 1830 and 1833, took part in sweeps against Japanese forces in the Bay of Bengal, becoming the first Corsair squadrons to operate in combat from an aircraft carrier.

On April 3, Corsairs from No. 1834 and 1836 squadrons participated in Operation *Tungsten*, a Fleet Air Arm raid to destroy the German battleship *Tirpitz* moored at Kafjord. FAA Corsairs operating from HMS *Victorious* were used as top cover for the pre-dawn strike, but met no enemy air opposition. The operation only managed to damage the German dreadnought, however. Operation *Goodwood* would be the final FAA attempt to destroy the *Tirpitz*, in which Corsairs participated. Two FAA Corsair squadrons, No. 1841 and No. 1842, flew top cover for the unsuccessful attacks.

On April 19, 1944, Corsair squadrons (No. 1830 and No. 1833) on board HMS *Illustrious* alongside aircraft from USS *Saratoga* took part in Operation *Cockpit*, targeting Japanese oil refineries and facilities on Sabang Island. Thirteen Corsairs would provide escort for FAA Barracudas while Hellcats from VF-12 escorted SBD Dauntlesses to the target. The FAA Corsairs took out a dozen Japanese aircraft on the ground. Additional FAA Corsair squadrons followed with the arrival of HMS *Victorious*.

On July 25, the FAA Corsairs were back in action as a dozen ships from Task Force 69 shelled the Japanese naval facilities on Sabang Island. FAA Corsairs provided both top cover for the task force and also aerial spotting to help adjust the naval gunfire. It was after the bombardment that British Corsairs finally met the enemy in the air. Corsair IIs from HMS *Illustrious* drew first blood for the FAA Corsairs; pilots from No. 1830 squadron destroyed three Zeros, followed by their sister squadron, No. 1833, claiming two more Zeros and a Ki-21 Sally. HMS *Victorious*'s No. 1838 claimed one Zero in the engagement. Additionally, a few of the Royal Navy Corsairs had cameras installed and were used for photo-reconnaissance and battle-damage assessments.

On October 19, 1944, Royal Navy Corsairs from HMS *Victorious* tangled with the Japanese. Corsairs from No. 1834 found enemy opposition over the Nicobar Islands. One Canadian FAA pilot, Lieutenant Leslie D. Durno, claimed three of the four Oscars shot down by No. 1834 squadron; two Corsairs were lost in the action. On January 4, No. 1843 and No. 1836 squadrons were participating in a raid against refineries on Pangkalan Brandan when enemy aircraft were encountered. Sub Lieutenant D. J. Sheppard (another Canadian flyer) of No. 1836 claimed his first two Oscars, while Lt Leslie Durno would also add to his score, claiming two shared kills. Seven aircraft in total were brought down by HMS *Victorious*'s Corsair squadrons without losing a Corsair. Eight aircraft were brought down on January 24 when the FAA aircraft participated in Operation *Meridian One* (a strike against refineries on Pladjoe, Sumatra). Four Corsair squadrons from both HMS *Illustrious* and *Victorious* were involved, flying both top cover and strafing and flak suppression missions. Sub Lt Sheppard claimed his third kill while Royal Marine aviator Major R. C. Hay brought down a Ki-43 and a Ki-44. One Corsair was shot down in air-to-air combat and another seven were destroyed from other causes. Five days later the FAA executed a raid against refineries on Soeni Gerong. On this day, Major Hay was coordinating the strike when he was jumped by Japanese fighters. Sheppard came to assist, and both pilots claimed one aircraft each. This was Hay's fifth kill of the war (three of which were made in a Corsair), making him the sole Royal Marine ace of the war.

Corsairs from HMS *Formidable*, *Illustrious*, and *Victorious* saw action at Sakishima in March, and in April participated in Operation *Iceberg* over Okinawa. The FAA Corsairs flew CAP missions and had knocked down five enemy aircraft by mid-month. Royal Navy carriers would not escape the kamikaze threat unscathed; however, when hit by the suicide aircraft, their armored decks limited the damage to the ship (aircraft on deck were another matter). On May 4, 1945, the FAA had its own Corsair ace when Lt Sheppard earned his fifth kill by shooting down a Japanese DY4 Judy. On August 9, 1945, the last FAA Corsair air-to-air kill was recorded, making a total of nearly 50 in three years of service. It was on this day that FAA Corsair pilot Lt Robert Hampton Gray earned the Victoria Cross (posthumously) while leading an attack on Japanese shipping around Onagawa Wan, Honshu. Antiaircraft fire from the ships hit his aircraft, but he continued on and released his bombs, which struck the Japanese ship *Amakusa*, sinking it. The young Canadian flyer was one of two FAA pilots to earn the Victoria Cross. A memorial was raised in Japan honoring the then-enemy pilot's courage. Corsairs did not remain long in FAA service, however. Due to the lend-lease agreement, if the FAA retained the leased aircraft they would have to pay for them; therefore most of the clipped-wing Corsairs were destroyed.

Royal New Zealand Air Force

In May 1944, the Royal New Zealand Air Force transitioned from the venerable Curtiss P-40 to the Vought F4U Corsair. By September 1945, the RNZAF had received a total of 424 Corsairs under the lend-lease program. Variants flown by the RNZAF included Vought-built F4U-1As, F4U-1Ds, and Goodyear-built FG-1Ds. Prior to receiving the Corsairs, the P-40 pilots had shot down a total of 99 aircraft. By the time the RNZAF started to convert to the F4U, most of the Japanese air activity around the northern Solomons from the earlier years had vanished. During the later stages of the war, the RNZAF was tasked with harassing bypassed islands. To manage this task the Corsairs were based all over the South Pacific. The RNZAF Corsairs were primarily for ground support missions. Escort and combat air patrols were flown, but with little chance of seeing Japanese aircraft. The RNZAF established 13 Corsair squadrons, numbered 14 through 26.

In all, the RNZAF lost 155 Corsairs of the 424 total received during the lend-lease program. Out of the 155 lost, only 17 were directly attributed to enemy action. The rest were operational and training losses. Number 14 Squadron would later serve in Japan for two-and a-half years on occupation duty. The squadron possessed two dozen FG-1Ds, operating from both Iwakuni and Bofu Japan. The unit's occupational duty came to a close in October 1948. Only a small number of Corsairs were ever returned to the USN, the majority being scrapped at the Rukuhia boneyard in New Zealand. The remaining Goodyear aircraft assigned to No. 14 Squadron were towed into a circle at Bofu and set ablaze.

Corsairs over Korea

A Naval Reserve F4U-4 flown by Lt Robert Pitner from VF-791 seen after attacking a bridge southwest of Wonson, Korea (background), 1951. VF-791 was stationed at NAS Memphis prior to being mobilized on July 20, 1950. VF-791 and her sister squadron VF-884 were the first Reserve Corsair squadrons to see combat in Korea, while serving aboard the USS *Boxer* (CV-21). (NMNA)

On June 25, 1950, North Korea invaded its neighbor to the south. The United States Navy responded by sending the USS *Valley Forge* to the region. After being readied for action, the *Essex*-class carrier launched her first strikes against North Korean airfields and rail yards located at Pyongyang on July 3, 1950. The strike consisted of F9F Panthers, AD-1 Skyraiders, and 16 F4U-4B Corsairs from VF-53 and VF-54; loaded with rockets, and the Corsairs hit their targets without losing an aircraft. Marine F4U-5P Corsairs from HEDRON-1, Detachment onboard the USS *Valley Forge* conducted battle-damage assessments of the initial strike on the same day. The first US Navy close air support mission was flown on July 22 in support of the Eighth Army. This was followed by an emergency CAS mission flown three days later; both missions had limited success. Problems emerged from disparities in radio equipment, maps, and also the definition of what close air support was in the first place. During the initial CAS mission, Navy Corsair pilots tried repeatedly to contact the Joint Operations Center (JOC) and USAF Mosquito aircraft operating as forward air controllers to no avail. Frustrated, the Corsairs and Skyraiders hunted targets on their own.

On August 3, 1950, the first Marine Corps offensive action of the war commenced. Eight Marine F4U-4Bs from VMF-214 launched from the USS *Sicily* at 1630, led by the squadron's executive officer, Major Robert P. Keller. The Corsairs executed napalm and strafing runs against troops in Chinju and Sinban-ni. The Blacksheep would soon be joined by VMF-323, "The Death Rattlers," who commenced combat sorties on August 6 from the deck of the USS *Badoeng Strait* (CVE-116). Both Corsair squadrons were assigned to Marine Air Group 33 (MAG-33) and continued their strikes in an effort to relieve pressure on General Walker's Eighth Army.

Close Air Support

The close air support situation saw a dramatic change with the entrance of the 1st Provisional Marine Brigade into the Korean War. The Marines were well trained in the use of combined arms, including utilizing close air support to its fullest. Corsair squadrons assigned to MAG-33 and later MAG-12 of the 1st Marine Air Wing were at a high state of readiness, and well-versed in their role to provide close air support prior to the war. The Navy-Marine CAS system had little red tape, allowing Corsair pilots to respond within a few minutes of being called. When not called upon by Marine units, the Corsairs furnished CAS for the Eighth Army and other UN forces, although Marine ground units had priority. Soldiers fighting alongside the Marines were amazed by the response times, accuracy, and proximity at which the CAS missions took place. As one Army Regimental Commander, Col Paul F. Freeman (USA), stated:

> The Marines on our left were a sight to behold. Not only was their equipment superior
> or equal to ours, but they had squadrons of air in direct support. They used it like
> artillery. It was 'Hey, Joe—this is Smitty—Knock the left off that ridge in front of Item
> Company.' They had it day and night. It came off nearby carriers, and not from Japan
> with only 15 minutes of fuel to accomplish the mission.

In August alone, USN and Marine Corsairs flew 6,575 combat hours. During the Battle of the Pusan Perimeter, Corsair squadrons from MAG-33 flew 1,511 sorties, with 995 of these being urgent CAS missions (Aug 3–Sept 14). In preparation for the upcoming Inchon landing, photo-reconnaissance missions were flown by F4U-5P Corsair pilots. Corsairs from VMF-214 and 323, as well as Navy Corsairs and Skyraiders from Task Force 77, decimated Inchon prior to the landings. All three Marine Corsair squadrons, alongside Navy Corsair squadrons, provided CAS during the landing. On September 18, ground forces took Kimpo Airfield; once the airfield was ready, additional Corsair Squadrons from MAG-12 arrived from Japan (VMF-212 and VMF-312). Marine Corsair squadrons moved north in support of the 1st Marine Division, operating from Wonsan and later from Yonpo Airfield in North Korea. The close air support system faced its greatest test in November and December 1950, as Chinese troops intervened. Both Marine and Navy Corsair squadrons played a crucial role in the 1st Marine Division's successful breakout from the Chosin Reservoir. The following is one day's account from VMF-312's diary:

On the first flight in the morning Major Avant and a flight of six planes worked with Devastate Baker Xray (a Marine R5D) in the Chosin Reservoir area and accounted for 200 hundred enemy troops killed, three buildings destroyed, and two trucks and one boat knocked out. All armament was expended on all flights during this day. Major Davis acted as Lovelace Playboy 1 and worked as a tactical air coordinator, directed 17 planes at the Chosin Reservoir. Capt Delong and his flight of four worked with Oxwood Playboy (TACA), and Capt Tery and his wingman worked with Splitseam Playboy (TACA) both flights hitting troop concentrations with results undetermined. Major Parker and his flight of four worked with Burner 14, a forward air controller, at Huksu-ri with the Third Army Division. This flight accounted for one tank, and two small vehicles. LtCol Cole (VMF-312's Commanding Officer) acted as a tactical air coordinator, in the afternoon, directing carrier AD's (Skyraiders) and Corsairs into targets for three hours.

(VMF-312 Historical Diary, Dec 4, 1950)

This F4U-5NL Corsair (BuNo 124525) assigned to VMF(N)-513 "Flying Nightmares" is armed with a mix of 6½-inch antitank aircraft rockets, incendiary bombs, and a Mk 77 napalm tank. A close inspection of this Corsair reveals the de-icing equipment on the propeller blades and leading edges of the wings and stabilizers. VMF(N)-513 flew a mix of night fighters during the Korean War including Corsairs, Grumman Tiger Cats, and Douglas Sky Knights. (NMNA)

Marine Tactical Air Control Parties (TACP) were placed at the battalion level all the way up to brigade HQs. Weather permitting, Corsairs would keep a continuous orbit over the division during daylight hours, with night fighters from VMF(N)-513 operating after dark. Corsair pilots utilized multi-channel radios to stay in contact with ground units. Corsair pilots acted as Tactical Air Coordinator Airborne (TACA, usually a two-ship formation) controlling strikes, utilizing 3.5-inch white phosphorus rockets to mark targets.

Medal of Honor over Chosin
The first African-American naval aviators for both the United States Navy and later the United States Marine Corps flew Corsairs during the Korean War. Ensign Jesse L. Brown, the first black naval aviator in US history, flew F4U-4s with VF-32 early in the Korean conflict. Brown was strafing Chinese troops near the Chosin Reservoir on December 4, 1950 when his aircraft (BuNo 97231) was brought down by enemy small-arms fire. Lieutenant Junior Grade (JG) Thomas J. Hudner flew over the downed aircraft and noticed that Brown was alive and trapped in the cockpit. Brown's legs had

FIRST MARINE OFFENSIVE STRIKE, KOREA, F4U-4B (BuNo 60367), VMA-214, USS SICILY (CVE-118) AUG 1950.
This F4U-4B Corsair BuNo 60367 assigned to VMF-214 waits to be launched from the deck of the USS Sicily CVE-118. On August 3, 1950, aviators from the Blacksheep Squadron of World War II fame successfully landed all 24 of their Corsairs on board the USS Sicily. Major Robert P. Keller, Executive Officer of the Blacksheep Squadron, was briefed shortly after coming on board and would lead the Blacksheep on their first combat mission since World War II. Eight of the squadron's Corsairs were immediately refueled and armed with a full complement of HVARs and one incendiary bomb each. At 1630, the Corsairs started launching from the Sicily's catapults in one minute intervals to take part in the first Marine airstrike of the Korean War. They headed towards their assigned target location in the southwest sector of Chinju. Aviators from VMF-214 successfully struck troop concentrations within the village, flattened buildings, and started numerous fires throughout the area without the loss of a single Corsair.

MEDAL OF HONOR CITATION, LIEUTENANT JUNIOR GRADE THOMAS J. HUDNER JR, USN

For conspicuous gallantry and intrepidity at the risk of his life above and beyond the call of duty as a pilot in Fighter Squadron 32, while attempting to rescue a squadron mate whose plane, struck by antiaircraft fire and trailing smoke, was forced down behind enemy lines. Quickly maneuvering to circle the downed pilot and protect him from enemy troops infesting the area, Lt (JG) Hudner risked his life to save the injured flier who was trapped alive in the burning wreckage. Fully aware of the extreme danger in landing on the rough mountainous terrain and the scant hope of escape or survival in subzero temperature, he put his plane down skillfully in a deliberate wheels-up landing in the presence of enemy troops. With his bare hands, he packed the fuselage with snow to keep the flames away from the pilot and struggled to pull him free. Unsuccessful in this, he returned to his crashed aircraft and radioed other airborne planes, requesting that a helicopter be dispatched with an ax and fire extinguisher. He then remained on the spot despite the continuing danger from enemy action and, with the assistance of the rescue pilot, renewed a desperate but unavailing battle against time, cold, and flames. Lt (JG) Hudner's exceptionally valiant action and selfless devotion to a shipmate sustain and enhance the highest traditions of the US Naval Service.

President Harry S. Truman presents Lt (JG) Thomas J. Hudner Jr of VF-32 with the Congressional Medal of Honor for his actions on December 4, 1950. Hudner intentionally crashlanded his Corsair near the downed aircraft of his flight leader, Ensign Jesse Brown, in order to try to free the aviator from the wreckage. (USN)

become entangled in the damaged instrument panel. Minutes later Lt (JG) Hudner purposely crashlanded his aircraft (BuNo 82050) near the crash site of Brown's Corsair and attempted to pull him out. Unable to free Brown, Lt Hudner called for a rescue helicopter. A Marine helicopter landed shortly thereafter with an axe and a fire extinguisher, as Hudner had requested. The pilots attempted to free Brown for 45 minutes in vain. Since the helicopter could not operate at night, there was nothing the pilots could do to save Brown (who by then was unconscious due to the severity of his wounds). Both Corsairs were later destroyed in an air strike in order to keep what was left of the crashed airframes out of enemy hands. Brown earned the Distinguished Flying Cross (posthumously); Lt (JG) Hudner earned the Congressional Medal of Honor for his selfless actions. Hudner never gave up on getting Brown out of North Korea; in July 2013 he visited Pyongyang in an attempt to gain permission to return to Chosin to locate Jesse Brown's remains and return them to the US.

Ordnancemen aboard the USS *Bunker Hill* (CV-17) rearm an F4U-1D with HVAR rockets prior to a mission over Okinawa. The F4U-1D and the Goodyear-built FG-1D were the first purpose-built fighter/bomber versions of the F4U Corsair. (National Archives)

Corsairs in Air-to-Air Combat over Korea

The Corsair's first aerial victory during the Korean War occurred on September 4, 1950. Radar on board the USS *Valley Forge* picked up a contact heading from the Russian naval base at Port Arthur, Manchuria, towards the Task Force. A division of F4U-4B Corsairs was vectored towards the contact, after which the radar operator observed the contact split in two, with a second aircraft turning back towards Port Arthur while the first aircraft continued on course. The VF-53 Corsairs intercepted a Soviet Navy Douglas A-20 only 30 miles out from the fleet. After spotting the Corsairs, the Soviet pilot dived and changed direction, heading toward North Korea. Lt (JG) Richard E. Downs, the division leader, continued to follow the intruder when the A-20's gunner opened fire. Downs reported back to the USS *Valley Forge* that the A-20 was firing on them, and received permission to fire. Downs fired but was out of position. Down's wingman, Ensign Edward V. Laney Jr, opened up with his four 20mm cannons and brought down the A-20.

The first Corsair aerial victory for the Marine Corps during the Korean War took place on April 21, 1951, when former World War II ace Captain Phillip DeLong (assigned to VMF-312) led a division on an armed reconnaissance mission. DeLong launched from the USS *Bataan* at 0540. Each Corsair in his division was armed with a 500lb bomb, drop tank, six HVARs (high velocity aircraft rocket) and two 100lb bombs. Two Corsairs from DeLong's division were detached to escort a rescue helicopter to pick up a downed aviator. DeLong and his wingman, Lt Harold D. Daigh, continued on with their mission. Daigh spotted four enemy aircraft at 5,000 feet; the silver-and-green camouflaged Yaks failed to see Daigh and attacked DeLong instead. DeLong's aircraft was hit, and he executed a "split S" manuever. Daigh went after them and found himself behind the third aircraft with the fourth now at his 7 o'clock. Daigh executed a 360-degree climbing turn, positioned himself behind two Yaks, and opened fire. He then attacked a Yak from 4 o'clock; the Yak's starboard wing broke off. A Yak crossed in front of DeLong's nose from left to right. He fired, sending the Yak out of control. He spotted Daigh chasing a Yak and noticed a second one about to gain position on Daigh's tail. DeLong radioed for Daigh to climb. Daigh turned sharp to port as the Yak overshot his position, then fired from below, scoring hits on the Yak, which was left smoking. DeLong then went after the lead Yak. The enemy pilot tried to evade him as DeLong scored hits, causing the plane to smoke. The enemy pilot went into a split S, but DeLong followed him and continued to put .50cal rounds into the fleeing Yak. The pilot bailed out and was seen landing in the ocean. DeLong radioed to have the rescue helicopter that was sent to pick up the downed Corsair pilot to come and pick up the Yak pilot. DeLong had smoke in the cockpit and Daigh's engine was giving him trouble. They both jettisoned their ordnance and landed back on the *Bataan* without incident. DeLong was credited with two Yak-9s and Daigh with one Yak-9 confirmed and one probable.

The first Marine Corsair kill at night during the Korean War was claimed by Capt Don L. Fenton of VMF(N)-513 "Flying Nightmares." On July 12, 1951, Capt Fenton was flying a F4U-5N when he was vectored towards a slow-flying bogey. Capt Fenton made visual contact with a Polikarpov Po-2, better known as "Bed-check Charlie," at 3,000 feet. Fenton opened up on the Po-2 from a range of 1,000 feet and observed the rear gunner returning fire as the right wings of the Po-2 disintegrated, followed by the fuselage exploding. On June 7, 1952, 1st Lt John W. Andre from the same squadron took off for an armed reconnaissance mission at 2125. The following shooting down of a Yak made him an ace with his combined score from his earlier victories in World War II:

The first African-American Marine Corps pilot, 2nd Lt Frank E. Petersen Jr, seen climbing out of an AU-1 Corsair. Petersen holds the distinction of not only becoming the first African-American Marine Corps aviator but the first African-American to command a Marine Corps flying squadron (VMFA-314, during the Vietnam conflict). He later became the first black general officer in the Corps. Petersen was assigned to VMA-212 in April 1953, one of only two Marine squadrons equipped with the AU-1 Corsair during the later stages of the Korean War. Petersen flew 64 combat missions in the AU-1, and earned the Distinguished Flying Cross and six air medals. (Marine Corps Historical Division)

I was making a run under flares on a convoy of trucks, I was at an altitude of 400 feet, course 270 degrees, speed 210 knots. A firing run was made on me by an enemy plane from the rear with tracers passing over my left wing, under the plane, and over the right wing. The enemy plane then passed me to starboard with an overtaking speed of 30-40 knots. He pulled up and to the right and I was able to get a silhouette of him against the sky about 3 o'clock. It was a single engine inline fighter-type aircraft, it appeared to be dark brown in color. I fired two bursts and flames immediately appeared from the underside of the plane, forward below the wings. The enemy plane seemed to try to pull up, but instead dove down and disappeared.

MiG-15 Kill

On September 10, 1952, Captain Jessie G. Folmar led a division of VMA-312 Corsairs from the USS *Sicily* on a strike mission; their target was 300 North Korean Army troops located four miles from the city of Chinamppo, on the south side of the Taedong River. Two Corsairs were tasked to cover a downed pilot, splitting Folmar's division. Folmar and his wingman proceeded to the target area but saw no enemy activity. They were in a weave formation three miles from Sock-To Island at 10,000 feet when Folmar spotted a pair of MiG-15s positioning themselves for a pass against the two Corsairs. Folmar turned into the MiGs while at the same time increasing power and jettisoning his ordnance. He reported that they were being attacked by MiGs over the guard channel, and had his wingman, Lt Willie L. Daniels, tighten up his defense. Folmar spotted a second pair of MiGs at his 8 o'clock position and turned in to them; the MiGs opened fire but missed. Folmar reverse-banked to the right and turned inside one of the MiGs, which then attempted to climb away. Folmar had him in his sights and gave him a five-second burst from his F4U-4B's (BuNo 62927) four 20mm cannons, scoring hits on the left side of the MiG-15's fuselage. Folmar witnessed the MiG starting to smoke; as the plane nosed over, the pilot ejected. Folmar and Daniels resumed their defensive weave when they spotted four more MiGs joining the fight. Folmar decided it was time to get out of there. He radioed Daniels and the two executed a 35-degree diving turn to port. Daniels saw a MiG on Folmar's tail; the MiG was able to score hits on Folmar's port wing, tearing off nearly four feet and gutting the top of it. Folmar bailed out soon after, transmitting his SAR (search and rescue) distress signal. The MiGs headed for home soon after an AA barrage opened up over Sock-To Island. Folmar was rescued after being in the water for eight minutes. Lt Daniels was able to get back to the USS *Sicily* with no damage to his Corsair. Folmar and Daniels had taken on eight MiG-15s and came away with each side losing one aircraft.

The Sole Navy Ace

Two F4U-5N pilots, Lt Guy P. Bordelon Jr and Lt (JG) Ralph Hopson, deployed from the USS *Princeton* to Kimpo Airfield near Seoul and later to Pyongtaek while working with Air Force controllers in June 1953. The pair of F4U-5N Corsairs from VC-3 Det 3 were utilized to patrol the UN frontlines against North Korean People's Air Force (NKPAF) nuisance raids. During his short assignment, Bordelon was credited with destroying two Yak-18s and three La-11 fighters during three separate missions. On each of the three missions, Bordelon was flying BuNo 124453, named ANNIE-MO for his wife.

The first mission took place during the early morning hours of June 30. When Bordelon and Hopson were vectored towards a hostile contact, Bordelon identified the contact as a Yak-18, a two-seat trainer used on night intrusions.

The aircraft's rear gunner opened fire in the wrong direction and Bordelon proceeded to destroy the Yak with his 20mm cannons. On the same mission, Boredelon's wingman had a malfunctioning radar, leaving Bordelon by himself when a second intruder was detected. Bordelon identified the second aircraft as another Yak-18 and brought it down. A few days later, Bordelon found himself in a similar situation; this time the contacts were identified by Bordelon as La-11s. It was on July 16 that the last aerial victory for a USN Corsair would take place, when Bordelon scored his final victory over a La-11, making him the sole Navy ace of the Korean War and the only non-jet ace. Bordelon earned the Navy Cross for his actions; his Corsair, ANNIE-MO, did not fare as well. An Air Force Reservist crashlanded BuNo 124453 soon after. The Air Force pilot survived; the aircraft was struck from the inventory.

The Navy's sole ace of the Korean War, Lt Guy P. Bordelon Jr, stands next to his F4U-5N Corsair (BuNo 124453) named "ANNIE-MO" for his wife. Bordelon would destroy five enemy aircraft while flying this aircraft. His Corsair was later scrapped after being involved in a accident while being flown by an Air Force Reservist. (Note the flame dampeners to conceal engine exhaust). (USN)

French Corsairs

The 14.F Flotille based at Karouba Air Base, Tunisia was the first squadron to receive the brand new F4U-7 on January 15 1953; however, the first Corsair type to see combat action with the French was not the F4U-7. On April 17, 1954, the squadron's personnel were deployed to Da Nang without their aircraft. The USS *Saipan* delivered 14.F Flotille's new aircraft the following day. Twenty-five veteran Marine AU-1 Corsairs, having formerly seen action during the Korean War, were to be used while the squadron awaited their F4U-7s. Of the 25 AU-1s delivered, however, only one was considered serviceable. In two days, maintenance personnel had 16 aircraft at Tourane ready to fly to Bach Mai Air Base. 14.F Flotille supported troops fighting during the collapse of Dien Bien Phu. On May 7, French forces at Dien Bien Phu surrendered to the Viet Minh, yet strike missions continued. On May 26, the squadron lost its first pilot to combat action; a second pilot was brought down on July 7. Combat missions ceased on July 21, 1954 after an international agreement was signed between Ho Chi Minh and the Republic of Vietnam, splitting the region.

During the two months of combat over Indochina, only two Corsairs were destroyed, with half a dozen others being damaged. The Corsair pilots from 14.F built an impressive combat record, dropping over 1.5 million pounds of bombs, firing over 300 rockets, and expending 70,000 20mm rounds. The AU-1 Corsairs were later returned to the US Navy. The French Navy obtained 57 additional AU-1s in 1957 and another dozen in 1958 when they became available. In 1956 the *Lafayette* returned to South Vietnam with Grumman TBF Avengers and Corsairs from 15.F Flotille onboard. These aircraft carried out the last mission over Vietnam for the French Aeronavale.

French Corsair squadrons also saw combat against Algerian guerillas, starting in 1956, and limited action in Tunisia in 1961. Flotilles 14.F and 15.F played a significant role during the Suez Crisis, after the nationalization of the Suez Canal by Egyptian President Gamal Abdel Nasser. French F4U-7 Corsairs were painted with black and yellow recognition stripes on the wings and fuselage prior to combat operations. The French Corsairs represented one-quarter of the carrier strike force involved in the conflict, with 36 aircraft

The F4U-7 was the last of the F4U Corsair line, built specifically for the French Aeronavale. The aircraft was essentially an AU-1 airframe with the engine from the F4U-4. This paired armor protection and payload carrying options similar to the AU-1 with the reliability and high-altitude performance of the F4U-4s R-2800-18W powerplant. (NMNA)

An F4U-5 (foreground) and an F4U-5NL (background) from the 2a Ecuadrilla Aeronaval de Ataque wearing vastly different paint schemes. Corsairs were known as Privateers while in service with Argentina. The Comando de Aviación Naval Argentina (COAN) flew Corsairs from both shore bases and the aircraft carrier ARA *Indepencia*. (Argentina)

available. On November 3, 1956, Corsairs launched from the carriers *Arromanches* and *Lafayette* to attack Cairo airport. During combat operations that lasted from November 1–7, only one F4U-7 was lost to combat action; BuNo 133711 was hit by antiaircraft fire over Cairo, killing L. V. Antoine Lancrenon, the squadron commander of 14.F. A second Corsair, BuNo 133728, was lost in a landing accident, although the pilot survived. F4U-7 Corsairs would continue to serve the French Aeronavale until the type's official retirement on September 28, 1964.

Latin American Bent Wing Birds

Honduras

The Honduran Air Force, or Fuerza Aerea Hondurena (FAH), was the first of three Latin American militaries to purchase Corsairs as part of the US Military Assistance Program. After the Korean War, Marine and Navy Corsairs started to become available in sufficient numbers. The Corsairs had a distinct advantage over other US types: due to continued production of the Corsair, many of the aircraft were relatively new, with fewer flying hours on them than other World War II-era aircraft. The Honduran government purchased a total of ten Corsairs in its initial order (four F4U-5N and six F4U-5NL night fighters). The Corsairs gained a solid reputation and were well-suited to deal with the hot climate and rugged terrain in Honduras. The Corsairs were less complicated to maintain and could outperform the older P-38s and P-63s already in FAH service. By 1959, the number of F4U-5 models available had dwindled, since Argentina had purchased 16 prior to Honduras's second order. As a result, the Honduran government purchased nine older F4U-4s, all delivered by 1961.

Argentina

Argentina purchased ten Corsairs through the US Military Assistance Program in 1956. All of the Corsairs were night fighters: four F4U-5Ns and six F4U-5NLs, delivered by 1957. The Corsairs were known as Privateers in Argentine service and were purchased for use by the Comando de Aviación Naval Argentina (COAN) in May 1956. In 1957, Argentina purchased another 16 F4U-5s and F4U-5NLs, most in flying condition, with a few utilized as spares. The Argentine Corsairs were formed into a single squadron, 2a Escuadra Aeronaval de Combate (later redesignated 2a Ecuadrilla Aeronaval de Ataque). The COAN Corsairs were received prior to Argentina's purchase of the ARA *Indepencia* (formerly HMS *Warrior*) in 1958. The ARA *Indepencia* was Argentina's first aircraft carrier. Corsairs from 2a Escuadra Aeronaval Ataque started operating from the *Indepencia* in June 1959, prior to the ship's official commissioning. When not operating from the carrier, the Corsairs were stationed on land bases. Many of the Argentinian F4U-5N and F4U-5NLs retained their night-fighter equipment. The COAN Corsairs could be utilized for both combat air patrols and ground support missions, but never

actually saw combat. The Comando de Aviación Naval Argentina disbanded its lone Corsair squadron in early 1966 and used the surviving airframes for training purposes.

El Salvador

In 1957 the El Salvadoran Air Force (Fuerza Aerea Salvadorena) followed Honduras's and Argentina's lead in procuring Corsairs through MAP. The FAS applied for F4U-5s, but Honduras (and later Argentina) had taken the majority of these late-model Corsairs, leaving El Salvador with few choices. In June 1957, the Fuerza Aerea

A Goodyear FG-1D, serial FAS-213 (BuNo 92618), of the Fuerza Aerea Salvadorena is being loaded with napalm. FAS Corsairs would have the misfortune of being victims in the last air-to-air engagement between piston-engine fighters. (Fuerza Aerea Salvadorena Museum)

Salvadorena purchased 20 Goodyear FG-1Ds, as there were sufficient numbers of this model to create a squadron. Of the 20 Corsairs, 15 were flyable, while the remaining five were to be used as spares. The FAS flew all 20 FG-1Ds and gave each its own unique serial number, designated FAS-201 through FAS-220. All of the Corsairs were assigned to the Escuadrilla de Caza, based at San Miguel. The FAS purchased five more Corsairs to try to slow the cannibalization rate; however, these F4U-4s had little in common with the older Goodyear aircraft. The Corsairs flew with the FAS until the summer of 1971. The older FG-1Ds were eventually replaced with Cavalier F-51D Mustangs IIs. Both of these types would see combat against the Honduran Air Force during the 100 Hours' War.

The 100 Hours' War

The 100 Hours' War (also known as the Soccer War) between El Salvador and Honduras was more complex than most press accounts of the time reported. Long-stemming economic, immigration, and political issues between the two countries came to a head during the summer of 1969. The war was labeled "The Soccer War" as tensions increased during a series of World Cup qualification matches between the two countries. On July 14, 1969, El Salvador initiated its attack with a series of air raids against Honduran cities. This was followed by El Salvadoran ground troops crossing the border into Honduras to take the town of Nacaome. A lone FAS C-47, used as a makeshift bomber, attacked the Honduran city of Toncontin. Honduran Air Force Corsairs were scrambled too late to catch the C-47 as darkness fell upon them. The Honduran F4U-5N Corsairs lacked standard night-fighter equipment, as most of it was removed well prior to the conflict.

Corsairs from both countries were used as fighter-bombers. On July 16, El Salvadoran troops occupied Nueva Ocotepeque. As soldiers continued their advance, they were assisted with close air support missions flown by a pair of FAS Goodyear Corsairs. On the 17th, a three-ship formation of HAF Corsairs lead by Major Fernando Soto Henriquez set off to attack enemy artillery positions. Soto, an experienced pilot with over 400 hours in the Corsair, had the group check their cannons. One of the F4U-5Ns had a malfunction and Soto ordered the pilot to return to Toncontin. As the pilot was returning to base, he was jumped by two FAS

This Vought F4U-5N (formerly BuNo 122179) is being ferried to the United States after being sold by the Fuerza Aerea Hondurena (FAH) in 1979 to Hollywood Wings. The FAH sold eight of the nine flyable Corsairs in their inventory. The one flyable Corsair retained by the FAH was serial FAH-609 that downed three Salvadorian Air Force aircraft in the 100 Hours' War. (NMNA)

Cavalier Mustangs. With his cannons jammed, the pilot radioed for help. Soto and his wingman heard the call, jettisoned their bombs, and rushed back to their endangered comrade. The lead FAS Mustang failed to score any hits on the F4U-5N. Soto spotted the Mustang pressing his attack and opened fire, scoring hits on the Mustang's fuselage. His wingman attacked the second F-51D. The pilot attempted to evade Soto, entering a diving turn below 800 feet. Soto followed, still firing at the Mustang, hitting the fuselage and wing. Soto managed to hit the engine, starting a fire. The F-51D (FAS-404) crashed into the woods. The second Mustang was able to evade Soto's wingman.

All three Honduran pilots made it back to their base. With their F4U-5Ns rearmed and refueled, they launched to eliminate an enemy artillery piece in the same area as their initial mission. The F4U-5N that had the earlier cannon malfunction was turned back a second time for the same reason. Nearing their target, Soto spotted a pair of FAS FG-1D Corsairs heading for home. He decided to pursue them, against standing orders not to cross into El Salvador. He scored hits on one of the Goodyears (FAS-204), forcing its pilot to bail out. The second FG-1D pilot was able to score hits on Soto's F4U-5N. Soto, utilizing the power advantage of the F4U-5N, was able to pull away and get behind the FG-1D (FAS-203). He opened fire, hitting the fuselage and cockpit of the FG-1D. Continuing his pursuit, he scored hits on the wings and the fuselage, sparking a massive explosion. This marked the last air-to-air engagement of piston-engine fighters in history. The war continued on for one more day until a ceasefire was established on July 18, 1969.

CONCLUSION

For a pre-World War II aircraft design to continue to see front-line service and to be produced in numbers well into the jet age speaks volumes about Vought's innovative design. The Corsair continued to set records throughout its career, from being the first single-engine aircraft to surpass 400mph, to having the longest production run of any piston-engine fighter in history. The Corsair was one of the first ship-borne fighters to outperform its land-based counterparts, similar to its archrival, the Mitsubishi A6M Zero. World War II aircraft are typically measured on the merits of their performance, lethality, durability, technological advances, and the number produced. The F4U Corsair would score well in any of these categories, but when one takes into consideration categories usually left out of the equation like longevity, mission diversity, adaptability, and timeliness, the Corsair is tough to beat. Also, head-to-head comparisons usually fail to take into account penalties incurred when an aircraft is designed to land and take off from a carrier: heavier gear, wing-folding mechanisms, and the limitations imposed on the aircraft's design by the carrier's own dimensions. The Fleet Air Arm seemed to understand this issue first hand, operating naval adaptions of the Hawker Hurricane and Supermarine Spitfire; both were truly great fighters, but lacked the design attributes to be considered great naval fighters.

The Corsair was not the fastest aircraft, nor was it the most maneuverable of the World War

An F4U-4 Corsair (BuNo 97369) on display at the National Museum of the Marine Corps in Triangle, Virginia. The Marine Corps Air-Ground Museum acquired the Corsair in 1975. The aircraft was restored in 2004 and placed on exhibit in the Museum's Leatherneck gallery in 2006. (Author's Collection)

II-era fighters. What the bent-wing bird gave the Allies was the most capable naval fighter of the war, in terms of both performance and adaptability. The United States Navy (who initially kept Corsairs off its carriers in 1943) later chose the F4U Corsair over the highly respected Grumman F6F Hellcat as the standard carrier fighter. This had a lot to do with the Corsair's performance as a fighter-bomber, something that both the Navy and Marine Corps still have within their inventories under different names (light-strike or multirole fighters) today. Corsairs could carry more ordnance than most World War II twin-engine bombers, and could fight their way in and out of the target area unescorted. The Corsair's availability during the Korean War saved countless lives on the front; in some of the most extreme operating locations, the Corsair could stay on station longer and could carry a heavier payload than the early Navy jets. As a testament to the Corsair's longevity, the last recorded Corsair air-to-air engagement took place at the same time as the Apollo 11 mission to the moon.

A pilot of an F4U-1D folds his Corsair's wings aboard the USS *Essex* (CV-9) after a strike mission against Kyushu, March 18, 1945. The USS *Essex* had three Corsair squadrons at the time, including the first Marine squadrons to operate from a CVE during the war, VMF-124 and VMF-213. (NMNA)

APPENDICES

Appendix A

Combat Operational Corsair Squadrons World War II	
United States Marine Corps (USMC)	**Royal Navy (Fleet Air Arm)**
VMF-111/112/113/114/115	No. 1830
VMF-121/122/123/124/155	No. 1833
VMF-211/212/213/214/215	No. 1834
VMF-216/217/218/221/222	No. 1836
VMF-223/224/225/251/311	No. 1841
VMF-312/313/314/321/322	No. 1842
VMF-323/351/422/441/451	No. 1838
VMF-452/511/512/513	
VMF(N)-532	**Royal Australian Air Force (RAAF)**
VMBF-231/331/333	No. 14
United States Navy (USN)	No. 15
VF-5/10/17/84/85	No. 16
VBF-1/6/10/83/85/86/88/94	No. 17
VF(N)-75/101	

Appendix B

Top 10 USMC/USN Corsair Aces		
Name	Squadron	Aerial Victories
Lt Robert M. Hanson	VMF-214/215	25
Maj Gregory Boyington	VMF-214	22
Capt Kenneth A. Walsh	VMF-124/222	21
Capt Donald N. Aldrich	VMF-215	20
Capt Wilbur J. Thomas	VMF-213	18.5

Lt Ira C. Kepford	VF-17	16
Capt Harold L. Spears	VMF-215	15
Capt Edward O. Shaw	VMF-213	14.5
Capt Philip C. DeLong	VMF-212/312	13.5
LCDR Roger R. Hedrick	VF-17/84	12

Note: All victories noted were accomplished while flying Corsairs: some pilots had additional kills while flying other types of aircraft.

Appendix C

USMC/USN Corsair Squadrons in Korea		
USMC Squadrons	Corsair Types	Tail Codes
VMF/VMA-214	F4U-4/B	WE
VMF/VMA-323	F4U-4/B, AU-1	WS
VMF-311	F4U-4B	WL
VMF/VMA-312	F4U-4/B	WR
VMF(N)-513	F4U-5N, F4U-5NL	WF
VMF/VMA-212	F4U-4/B, F4U-5, F4U-5N, AU-1	LD
VMJ-1	F4U-5P	MW
VMA-332	F4U-4/B	MR

Note: Some squadrons used a mixture of aircraft types. For example, VMF(N)-513 also flew Grumman Tigercats and Douglas Skyknights along with Corsairs. Also, headquarters and maintenance squadrons also had various Corsair types assigned.

Corsair Variants by Squadron	
Squadrons	Corsair Types
USN VF Squadrons 53,54, 871,23,63,64,65,24,44, 783,874,74,32,33,884,144,874, 713, 192,193, 821,871, 152, 653,194,92,113,114,94	F4U-4, F4U-4B
VC Squadron Detachments 3, 4, 62, 61	F4U-5N/NL, F4U-5P, F4U-4P

Appendix D

Post World War II Aerial Victories						
Date	Squadron	Aircraft Flown	Pilot	Weapon	Enemy Aircraft Destroyed	Number
4/09/50	VF-53	F4U-4B	Ens Edward V. Laney Jr.	20mm	A-20*	1
21/4/51	VMF-312	F4U-4	Lt Harold D. Daig	.50cal	Yak-9	1
21/4/51	VMF-312	F4U-4	Capt Phillip C. DeLong	.50cal	Yak-9	2
12/7/51	VMF(N)-513	F4U-5N	Capt Donald L. Fenton	20mm	Po-2	1
7/6/52	VMF(N)-513	F4U-5N	Lt John W. Andre	20mm	Yak-9	1
10/09/52	VMA-312	F4U-4B	Capt Jesse G. Folmar	20mm	MiG-15	1
30/6/53	VC-3 DET D	F4U-5N	Lt Guy P. Bordelon Jr	20mm	Yak-18	2
1/7/53	VC-3 DET D	F4U-5N	Lt Guy P. Bordelon Jr	20mm	La-11*	2
16/7/53	VC-3 DET D	F4U-5N	Lt Guy P. Bordelon Jr	20mm	La-11*	1
17/7/69	FAH	F4U-5N	Capt Ferdinand Soto	20mm	F-51D	1
17/7/69	FAH	F4U-5N	Capt Ferdinand Soto	20mm	FG-1D	2

*Note: Official Navy records state that an Il-4 was destroyed on September 4, 1950 instead of a Douglas A-20 Boston. USN records also state Lt Guy Bordelon shot down three Po-2s instead of La-11 fighters. The pilot stated the aircraft in these three encounters were La-11s.

SELECT BIBLIOGRAPHY

Barrett, Tillman, *Corsair*, Naval Institute Press (Annapolis, Maryland, 1979)

Blackburn, John Thomas, and Hammel, Eric, *The Jolly Rogers, The Story of Tom Blackburn and Navy Fighting Squadron VF-17*, Orion Books (New York, 1989)

Boyington, Gregory, *Baa Baa Blacksheep*, Bantam (1977)

Condon, John R., and Mersky, Peter B., *Corsairs to Panthers: US Marine Aviation in Korea*, U.S. Marine Corps Historical Center (Washington, DC, 2002)

Dorr, Robert F., Marine Air: *The History of the Flying Leathernecks in Words and Photos*, Berkley Publishing Group (New York, 2005)

Elliott, John M., *Marine Corps Aircraft 1913-2000 Occasional Paper*, History and Museums Division Headquarters, US Marine Corps (Washington, DC, 2002)

Gamble, Bruce, *The Black Sheep: The Definitive Account of Marine Fighting Squadron 214 in World War II*, Random House Publishing Group, New York (1998)

Guyton, Boone, T., *Whistling Death: The Test Pilot's Story of the F4U Corsair*, Schiffer Publishing Ltd (Atglen, Pennsylvania, 1994)

Harvey, Ralph, *Developing the Gull-Winged F4U Corsair and Taking it to Sea*, Ralph Harvey, (2012)

Larkins, William T., *US Navy Aircraft 1921–1941: US Marine Corps Aircraft 1914–1959*, Orion Books (New York, 1961)

Masatake, Horikoshi Jiro, and Caidin, Martin Okumiya, *The Zero Fighter*, Cassell Publishing (1956)

Moran, Gerald P., *Aeroplanes Vought 1917-1977*, Historical Aviation Album (Temple City, California, 1978)

Petersen, Frank E., and Phelps, J. Alfred, *Into the Tiger's Jaw: America's First Black Marine Aviator*, Naval Institute Press (Annapolis, Maryland, 1998)

Peterson, Bernard W., *Short Straw Memoirs of Korea*, Chuckwalla Publishing (Scottsdale, Arizona, 1996)

Pitzl, Gerald R., *A History of Marine Fighter Attack Squadron 323*, History and Museums Division Headquarters, US Marine Corps (Washington, DC, 1987)

Sambito, William J., *A History of Marine Fighter Attack Squadron 311*, History and Museums Division Headquarters, US Marine Corps (Washington, DC, 1978)

Sambito, William J., *A History of Marine Fighter Attack Squadron 312*, History and Museums Division Headquarters, US Marine Corps (Washington, DC, 1978)

Shaw Jr, Henry I., and Donnelly, Ralph W., *Blacks in the Marine Corps*, History and Museums Division Headquarters, US Marine Corps (Washington, DC, 2002)

Sherrod, Robert, *History of Marine Corps Aviation in World War II*, Combat Forces Press (Washington, DC, 1952)

Styling, Mark, *Corsair Aces of World War 2* Osprey Publishing (London, 1996)

Swanborough, Gordon, and Bowers, Peter, M., *United States Navy Aircraft since 1911*, Naval Institute Press (Annapolis, Maryland, 1982)

Thompson, Warren, *F4U Corsair Units of the Korean War*, Osprey Publishing (Oxford, 2009)

United States Navy, *Standard Aircraft Characteristics for all USN/ USMC Models of the F4U Corsair*

Veronico, Nicholas A., and Campbell, John M. and Donna, *F4U Corsair: Combat, Development, and Racing History of the Corsair*, Motorbooks International Publishers & Wholesalers (Osceola, Wisconsin, 1994)

Vought F4U Corsair Famous Airplanes of the World Special Edition Volume 5, Burindo Co. Ltd (Nakano-ku, Tokyo,Japan, 2010)

Wolf, William, *Death Rattlers: Marine Squadron VMF-323 Over Okinawa*, Schiffer Military History (Atglen, Pennsylvania, 1999)

Young, Edward M., *American Aces against the Kamikaze*, Osprey Publishing (Oxford, 2012)

INDEX

Figures in **bold** refer to illustrations.